STARTLED BY GOD

WISDOM FROM UNEXPECTED PLACES

JOE MCHUGH

Franciscan
MEDIA
Cincinnati, Ohio

Unless otherwise designated, Scripture references are taken from the *New Revised Standard Version of the Bible*, copyright © 1989 by the Division of Education of the National Council of Churches of Christ in the U.S.A., and are used with permission. All rights reserved. David Foster Wallace's commencement address at Kenyon College was published in the *Wall Street Journal*, September 19, 2008. All quotations from the *Spiritual Exercises of St. Ignatius Loyola*, are from *The Spiritual Exercises*, Spanish and English, Joseph Rickaby, S.J., London, 1923. "Getting on the Bus," "Hockney's Pool," "Holding Hands with God," and "What God Looks Like" have been adapted from shorter articles first appearing in the *National Catholic Reporter*. Reprinted by permission of *National Catholic Reporter*, 115 Armour Blvd., Kansas City, MO 64111-1203, NCRonline.org. The essay "Is God Happy?" appears in *Is God Happy? Selected Essays*, Leszek Kołakowski, Basic Books, New York, NY, 2013.

Cover and book design by Mark Sullivan
Cover image © benoitb | istockphoto.com

LIBRARY OF CONGRESS CATALOGING-IN-PUBLICATION DATA
McHugh, Joe.
Startled by God : wisdom from unexpected places / Joe McHugh; [foreword by] Michael Joncas.
pages cm
1. Spirituality—Christianity. I. Title.
BV4501.3.M345 2013
242—dc23
2013025777
ISBN 978-1-61636-685-8

Published by Franciscan Media
28 W. Liberty St.
Cincinnati, OH 45202
www.FranciscanMedia.org

Printed in the United States of America.
Printed on acid-free paper.
13 14 15 16 17 5 4 3 2 1

For Francis Kline
Monk of Mepkin Abbey
1948–2006
R.I.P.

"The really important kind of freedom involves attention, and awareness, and discipline, and effort, and being able truly to care about other people and to sacrifice for them, over and over, in myriad petty little unsexy ways, every day. That is true freedom."

—David Foster Wallace
Commencement Address,
Kenyon College, 2005

| CONTENTS |

My initial instinct in agreeing to write this foreword for Joe McHugh's book, *Startled by God: Wisdom from Unexpected Places*, was to take the usual academic approach. I would identify the genre of writing (practical spirituality) by comparing the work to others in the field (Margaret Silf, Mary Margaret Funk, Thomas Merton, David Steindl-Rast). I would then point out what is distinctive about this author's contribution: for example, the varying importance of ideas, stories, and images in the spiritual journey; the concept of "spiritual binocularity;" the organizing categories of "what," "so what," "now what;" the rich mining of Ignatian insights in contemporary language and imagery. I would conclude by recommending the book to a particular readership: adults who are serious but not stuffy about their spiritual lives, who are willing to risk discovering new things about themselves, their world, and their God.

But this approach could not do justice to Joe's book. The voice you will encounter in these pages is so personal, so authentic, that I feel challenged to be equally personal in expressing why I think *Startled by God* is such a gem. And to do that I have to make a slight detour to speak about my own encounters with Joe.

After five decades of studying the classics of Western and Eastern spirituality, after committing myself as a priest in 1980 to the frequent celebration of Mass and the Liturgy of the Hours, after giving myself over to the practice of the Jesus Prayer for at least ten years in the 1990s, after practicing *lectio divina* faithfully in preparing the preaching I would do at Lord's Day Eucharist, and after having my entire world turned upside down in 2003–2004 when I contracted Guillain-Barré Syndrome (leading to months of almost complete paralysis and subsequent physical recovery), I had reached a dead end. While I continued to minister and teach out of what I knew in faith to be true, my interior life was bleak and empty. The God I knew was silent and distant, and I could find no techniques or methods that would give me any sense of contact with the divine. I stayed as faithful as I could to the spiritual disciplines I had undertaken, but I had almost no experience of God that I could identify.

I confided my situation to one of my longtime priest friends. He recommended that I contact Joe McHugh to see if he would serve as a spiritual director for me. I have now had the privilege of sharing my interior life with Joe about once a month for some years. Without exaggeration, I can testify that through those conversations and the suggestions Joe has offered, I have rediscovered and entered into a new relationship with God.

Joe is fiercely intelligent (notice the teachers and mentors he mentions and the authors he quotes), but wears his learning lightly. He is appropriately self-disclosive, as a fellow disciple on the Way sharing what he has learned of God. He has a quirky sense of humor, frequently directed at his own foibles. He observes humanity in all of its variety with the eye of an artist and the heart of a poet. Best of all, he is authentic: The world he inhabits is recognizably real, the world of Starbucks and smart phones, CPAs, and Ten Thousand Villages. It is in this real world that he finds God alive and active and invites us to do the same.

So prepare yourself to be charmed and to wrestle with these essays. (Don't try to read the book in one sitting.) You will hear marvelous conversations going on among Joe's experiences, the stories of people he has met and observed, and the world of the Scriptures, modeling for us ways to identify the action of God in our own lives. Do the homework Joe suggests in many of the essays to become a partner in this conversation.

Though Joe would be embarrassed to hear me say it, *Startled by God* is a work by a genuine spiritual guide in the Ignatian tradition speaking directly to contemporary people, someone with hard-won and eloquent wisdom in the ways of God and humanity. Don't be surprised if God uses the ideas, stories, and images you will find within to change your life as they have changed (and are changing) mine.

Fr. Jan Michael Joncas
Feast of St. Mark, April 25, 2013
St. Paul, Minnesota

| ACKNOWLEDGMENTS |

I want to thank Mary Carol Kendzia, my editor, for suggesting this book in the first place and leading me through its development. She knows how to suggest without intruding. Although I'm no theologian, I've been lucky to study with the best of them. Avery Dulles, S.J., showed me how a theologian thinks, and Leo J. O'Donovan, S.J. introduced me to the theology of Karl Rahner, while teaching me that theology could also be beautiful. Walter L. Farrell, S.J., Frank J. Houdek, S.J., and Rita Anne Houlihan, R.C., true companions of Jesus, taught me more about spiritual direction than they know. I am forever in their debt.

—Easter Sunday, 2013

I worked in the library at the Catholic college I attended, and my job was putting books back on the shelves after they were returned. One late afternoon, while working, I discovered a section of books labeled "restricted"—which was all the motivation I needed to sort carefully through them. That's when I found a book that grabbed my attention: *Shepherds in the Mist*. Since I couldn't take it out, I read it during my breaks until I finished it.

E. Boyd Barrett, an English Jesuit, wrote this book in 1949, and it told about—and here I'll approximate his language—his seduction by blinding passion and his shameful defection from the Jesuit order. Sin and guilt condemned him to wander in the mist of ignorance and shame until grace finally returned him to his senses, and he once again took up the vocation God had willed for him.

Since I left the Jesuits after twenty years in the order, I probably qualify as a member of the Shepherds in the Mist Club. But unlike Fr. Barrett, I don't think God wanted me to spend my whole life as a Jesuit. God had other plans.

I loved my years as a Jesuit. I was afforded countless opportunities for education, growth, and service, and I lived with genuinely holy men, quietly intent on helping souls. But entering and leaving the Jesuits were the two best decisions I ever made: God was in them both. I also lived with the Trappist monks at Gethsemani Abbey in Kentucky, feeling more at home there than with the Jesuits.

While my imagination belonged to the Jesuits and my heart to the Trappists, the world finally captured my life. Unlike Fr. Barrett, the mist turned out to be a place of insight, faith, and growth for me. Only after leaving religious life did I experience the real power of the retreat experience St. Ignatius Loyola captured in his little book, the *Spiritual Exercises*, a reliable sign that my real vocation lay outside the Jesuits. Living in a monastic community gave me an interesting take on Ignatian spirituality, but my life in the world transformed both experiences.

I continued doing spiritual direction and giving retreats after I left the Jesuits, and I have shared stunning stories of grace and growth with amazing people — lay, religious, and priests — in the process. My recent grace has been teaching what I've learned about spirituality and spiritual direction with Protestant folks and their pastors.

Spiritual direction is nothing if not reflecting and praying with another person about opportunities God is always offering us to be more fully alive in the concrete stories of our lives. That's where we're often startled to find God waiting patiently and lovingly in unexpected places. We just need to keep our eyes, ears, and lives open to faith, hope, and love — the heart of Christian living and spiritual direction.

Startled by God: Wisdom from Unexpected Places is a collection of brief stories about how God camps out in our lives, particularly in those dusty corners of experience where we've frantically posted "no trespassing" signs, secretly hoping to keep God at a cordial yet uninvolved distance. In my case, God has always offered a helping hand when I was ready to take tentative steps into trust. Although this book is personal, I hope you'll see traces of your own story with God in what I write.

Stories and images—the stuff of spiritual direction—keep us anchored in real life, rather than in hollow abstractions or disembodied theological niceties. My basic assumption is that while ideas can inform us and stories can change us, only images can heal us.

But why stories and images? Because they give us access to the heart of life by showing rather than telling, creating pictures that help us see and feel, not just understand. That's why we remember them, and it's also why Christians read Bible stories over and over until we finally start seeing the same story of healing and hope in the twists and turns of our own stories of life with God.

God is an eternal storyteller, always at work on a divine epic of mercy, creativity, and gracious love. Luckily, God has included our own stories as subplots in that great drama. God's story and our own life stories crisscross, intersect, and aren't complete without each other. That's real gospel—good news—what God and grace and life are all about.

As it turns out, God only tells one story: how we are constantly offered ways of being so fully alive that we can describe the experience only as eternal life. But God tells that one story using a variety of themes such as death and resurrection, nothingness and creation, healing and health, exclusion and inclusion. God delights in offering us real life, full life, eternal life.

The book of Genesis shows us how God created out of nothing. Don't we see the same story when God raises Jesus out of the supposed nothingness of death? Isn't it also the story we see when Jesus gives sight to the blind, hearing to the deaf, or clean skin to lepers? What's most startling of all is how often God is at work in those parts of our experience we often write off as dead ends. These are the places I'd like to explore with you in this book.

| OUR WAY OF PROCEEDING |

The early Jesuits used the expression "our way of proceeding" to describe how they went about things. It had less to do with practical procedures to get things done than with the habits of mind and heart that gave real life to their undertakings. And so I'd like to suggest a way of proceeding together through this book. I want you to know the practicalities of how this book is organized, but, even more, I'd also like to suggest habits of mind and heart that might help the book come alive for you.

I've loosely organized the stories in *Startled by God* around three questions used in a well-known method of collaborative inquiry: what? so what? now what? In other words, the three questions are about how we describe, interpret, and act on experience. Adapt these questions slightly, and they can help structure a conversation in spiritual direction: How is God active in your life? What does God's activity mean to you? How might you respond appropriately?

Also, the word *dilemmas* is used deliberately in each of these sections. Dilemmas confront us with choices and alternatives, and they need to be managed, not solved. And managing dilemmas is perhaps a good way to describe discernment—that is, sifting through choices and alternatives and looking for traces of real grace in at least one of them.

The stories in part one, then, are about dilemmas of perspective. How do we imagine—for better or ill—our relationship with God, self, and others? I'll also suggest how an either/or perspective can be limiting or even harmful.

The stories in part two are about dilemmas of discipleship. How do we interpret the challenges we inevitably face in our resolve to be disciples of Jesus? Let's face it, although this is an overarching direction in Christian discipleship—our gradual incorporation into life with God in Jesus—none of us is issued a pregame playbook that outlines exactly what challenges we'll face and how to handle them. To make things even more complicated, few of the challenges we face as disciples happen on cue; there's often a random feel to what we experience, when we experience it, and what to make out of it.

The stories in this section will undoubtedly have a similar feel. That's why I'll also suggest a variety of prayer practices in this section. Prayer helps us embrace and integrate what we experience in the mysterious working of grace. Connecting the dots is often like the connect-the-dots puzzles we did as kids; only at the end can we look back and say, "Of course."

The stories in part three are about dilemmas of discernment. How do we make sense out of all the desires, impulses, and possible ways of acting we face as disciples? Which seem to come from God and lead to life, and which come from other sources of personal and social influence and lead us away from God? Unfortunately, there can be even more confusion involved in this process. What seems to come from God but really doesn't? What are we convinced can't be from God, but, in the end, really is? Don't look for a clear road map of where to go and what to do. The best I can offer are tentative directions.

You'll find questions for reflection and suggestions for journaling (or simply writing) in many of the stories—but not all. I did this intentionally, hoping that as you read these stories, you will get an idea of how to frame questions for reflection that come from your experience, not mine. Use the technique of asking what, so what, and now what to help you in this process.

Ignore the questions and you may wind up reading this book only for information, possibly bypassing the deeper needs of heart and soul. Even better, read the book with another person or a group, using the "what, so what, and now what" questions to guide your conversations, reflections, and practices. Doing so is also a way to make real our belief that Jesus is present and active among those gathered in his name.

The real heart of our way of proceeding, however, is doing all of this with an interior openness—a willingness to be startled by God—and with prayer. Prayer is a way in which God can deal with us directly, giving the story of our lives a chance to mix with God's great, silent story of gracious, forgiving love. Please also be assured that I would feel privileged to talk with you as you read, reflect, and pray. You can contact me through my website, www.spiritualdirectiontwincities.com.

PART ONE

WHAT?

Dilemmas

of

Perspective

There's a wonderful story about late American Jesuit theologian Cardinal Avery Dulles that is no doubt as apocryphal as it is charming. He supposedly once slipped into a church and spied a banner hanging from the pulpit that read, "God Is Other People." After checking to make sure the coast was clear, he took a marker from his pocket and inserted a comma in the wording that made it read, "God Is Other, People."

Tucked away in the story's humor is a permanent tension in how Christians understand and experience God. God utterly transcends anything we can think, know, or imagine—God Is Other, People—and God is also intimately present in our experience, particularly in human relationships—God Is Other People.

We live on a spiritual continuum between the two. We long for bread and are given living bread, for life and are given eternal life, for a shepherd and are given the Good Shepherd. But without ordinary bread, ordinary life, and an ordinary shepherd, the eternal depth of God's grace is nowhere to be found.

We grow as human persons when we have an image of who we are and who we hope to become, coupled with a compelling story that gives real light to our path. Without image and story, our lives turn into little more than a collection of disconnected episodes in search of a plot. Our growth as Christians follows a similar path. Until we find an image of God that enlivens our imaginations and quickens our hearts, our spiritual lives are a cluttered collection of experiences in search of substance and sustenance.

Let me give you an example. In 1958 my parents bought a self-portrait of an Ohio painter, Emerson Burkhart; it hung in our living room for the next thirty years. During that time, Emerson probably plugged his ears when I practiced piano, but he also shared Christmas celebrations, refereed bridge games, and silently held us in his gaze as we planned my father's funeral. I inherited the portrait in 1989, and it's hung in my living room ever since. Emerson has seen me grow up and is now watching me grow old in his protective, calming sight.

You and I share a DNA-deep desire to be seen as special and lovable by someone significant. When this happens, we can finally take our place with the rest of creation as "very good" in God's sight, and our world becomes a place of grace and hope rather than one of danger and threat.

I start my prayer every morning in Emerson's sight. He's become a powerful image of God for me, an icon of God's benevolent oversight, without which I can be tempted to let selfish isolation hijack my soul. Like people in the Gospels, we are made whole only in the healing sight of the God we recognize in Jesus. Emerson is a face I can put on Jesus that shows me what God is like.

Allowing Emerson's image to remind me of God's love also helps me see what goes on around me with new depth. For example, I often see a mother bring her visually and mentally challenged adult son to Starbucks for a treat on Sunday afternoons. While there, they reach for one another's hands, wordless reassurance, it seems, that they are both still there for each other. Who doesn't need to be reassured that we've not been abandoned or left to die? We probably surround ourselves with pictures of friends and family for the same reason.

Each year we celebrate the Baptism of the Lord, and our attention is drawn to what the words and actions in that story say about God, Jesus, and us (Mark 1:9–11). When John baptizes Jesus, the heavens open, the Spirit descends, and a voice describes Jesus as God's beloved, someone in whom God takes delight.

Our image of God needs to be rooted in this story, because we find our real life when we hear God speak the same words into our hearts: You are also my beloved in whom I delight. My praying and living under the loving gaze of Emerson Burkhart comes with a depth that finds final expression and completion in a Gospel story like this. In the end, both images merge and yet both remain distinct. This is the great mystery of all love, human and divine.

Spend some time remembering or searching for your own image of God, something you keep coming back to because it speaks so deeply to your heart about the nature of God. It might be a person in whose gaze you feel safe and occasionally even challenged, or a Bible story that always shows you what God must be like. When you remember it or find it, enjoy it as God's beloved. This is your place with God, in which your prayer starts and your life finds a loving home.

My birthright is second-class vision. I can't remember a time without glasses, and McHugh family lore holds that I even asked my mom if I had glasses on when I was born. I can't remember what she said, but I do know that my eyesight has always been just good enough to get and keep a driver's license.

A week or so before I started college, I had my eyes examined by an ophthalmologist I had never gone to before. He was smart and professional, and had a soft-spoken manner about him. But if you listened carefully to what he said, it was fairly clear that this guy flunked Bedside Manner 101.

"You've got terrible binocularity," he said, "and that's why you have a bad case of imperfect stereopsis." Since he used two interesting words I'd never heard before, I interrupted his spiel to find out what they meant.

"You don't use both eyes; that's why you've got borderline depth perception." He sounded downright irked with my question, but he went on. "'Imperfect stereopsis' means that since your eyes don't work together, they don't come together in a single point on the horizon right in front of you. That's why you have trouble calculating how far things are away from you." I sort of understood, but I bit my tongue, not daring to ask another question.

"If you get a job that requires lots of reading," he snapped, "it would be like somebody with a clubfoot going out for track." Just the encouragement I needed right before I packed up for college. It galls me to say it, but he was right. I use only my right eye to see. If I squint, I can use my left eye by itself, but I never use them both together. You might say I have either/or rather than both/and vision. Whenever blindness comes up in Scripture, it's usually a metaphor for spiritual blindness, or what we might call imperfect spiritual depth perception. When Jesus gives sight to the blind, their physical eyes are opened, but so are the eyes of their heart. If we take these stories as metaphors for our own spiritual blindness, we'll soon discover our own need to make our way to Jesus to have our spiritual sight restored, or at least deepened.

Keep in mind that how we see is often just as important as what we see. How we see something determines how we understand it, and seeing something clearly for what it is—on its own terms, not ours—helps us discern its personal meaning for us. How we see God and self, prayer and discipleship, love and service, is crucial for living a Gospel life.

We can suffer from imperfect spiritual binocularity. Some of us can only see our grace or our guilt, but we rarely see them together. Others see only death or resurrection, loss or gain, sacred or secular, real life or spiritual life, business life or religious life, self-giving or self-fulfillment. As a result, we see with little spiritual depth because these seemingly irreconcilable experiences never meet in the merciful heart of our God, the Holy Mystery at the deepest and most central point of our personal horizon.

We need Jesus to smear our eyes with mud and spittle to heal our damaged spiritual vision—the one-sided way we might see God and ourselves. Our gift, however, is in seeing ourselves with both eyes. That's when we see ourselves as God sees us: a loved sinner.

We have to keep telling ourselves that we have a both/and rather than either/or God. As our spiritual binocularity starts to heal, we see guilt and grace, death and resurrection, loss and gain, giving and receiving, and sacred and secular in a single vision that is not only healthy, but also saving.

We need to make regular appointments with God to have the eyes of our heart examined, and, when necessary, change the prescription for our glasses. Allowing our injured eyes to be healed in the loving gaze of Jesus keeps God and grace as part of our lived experience, not just polite ideas. All we can do is bring our either/or vision in prayer to Jesus for continual healing over time.

Take time to page through the Gospels and read some of the stories about Jesus opening the eyes of the blind. Read these stories slowly and meditatively so Jesus can also touch and heal you. Are you drawn to one story in particular? If so, what is it that draws you in and what might it mean for you?

My brother, Kevin, and I went to school in rural Ohio at the height of the Cold War. Godless communism was our clear enemy, and I still remember sitting at the kitchen table writing a paper about J. Edgar Hoover's book about the subject, *Masters of Deceit*, as the final paper in government class my senior year in a public high school.

We came at communism from a decidedly different perspective when we were in Catholic elementary school. Our principal, Sr. Theophane, visited each classroom each month telling us how blood would flow down our streets when the communists took over. The only way we could fight off disaster, she told us, was by saying the rosary every day, wearing the scapular, wearing modest clothes, and staying pure—not much of a challenge for an eight-year-old.

Jesus seemed to get short shrift in our religious training. Instead, Mary got top billing; she was the only one, we were told, who could hold back God's rage. But time was running out. She could hold back God's rage for only so long before God's white-hot anger would breach its boundaries and we'd all be annihilated. Now there's a scary image of God: If you don't love me, you'll get wasted.

Kevin and I made the mistake of telling the "blood flowing down our streets" story one night at dinner, at which point our dad—thank God for islands of sanity—threatened to pull us out of Catholic school if we ever repeated a story like that again. Needless to say, we kept our mouths shut when we learned the next month we'd be eating eyeball soup when the communists seized control.

When our pastor, Fr. Florian Hartke, celebrated his twenty-fifth anniversary as a priest, Sr. Theophane hatched a plan to give him the spiritual gift of a lifetime. All of us were told to join the Blue Army of Our Lady of Fatima or risk getting kicked out of school. Naturally, we all signed the pledge card, thinking it would be cool to have them flown to Portugal and buried at Mary's feet. When he received his gift, Fr. Hartke pretended to be overjoyed, but when I actually got to know him years later, it was clear he would have preferred golf balls as a gift.

Don't be fooled into thinking that this kind of theology died an appropriate death when the Soviet Union fell, because it's still alive and still deadly. Plenty of people tried to convince us that Hurricane Katrina was divine retribution for sin, and a local pastor announced that Minneapolis was hit by a tornado because the Lutheran Church in America decided to ordain practicing homosexuals.

I'm not telling these stories to be flippant or smart-alecky, but rather as a serious invitation to ask ourselves why so many Christians find the image of a vindictive, punishing God so addictively compelling. Underneath it all lurks one big gnawing question: How do we manage our sense of guilt, sin, fear, and shame in a way that it doesn't savage our sense of being good, if not perfect, in God's sight?

In the first exercise of the *Spiritual Exercises*, St. Ignatius Loyola invites persons making the retreat to place themselves at the foot of the cross and pray there. Many saints, certainly Ignatius Loyola and Francis of Assisi, saw the cross less as a sign of atonement for human wrongdoing than as an arresting symbol of God's overwhelming, personal love for us.

It's love alone that elicits genuine sorrow for sin because it drives out fear to make room for forgiveness and hope. Irrational guilt, it turns out, can inspire compliance, not love. As we approach the cross, weighed down with our guilt and shame, God's grace alone can transform them at the same time into genuine sorrow and inspire an authentic openness to the gift of forgiving love. We find our true spiritual identity as a loved sinner—nothing more, nothing less.

As sophisticated as I think I am and as smart as the people are with whom I talk in spiritual direction, the strident voices of guilt and shame we are convinced we outgrew years ago still demand airtime in our hearts from time to time. That's a sure sign we need to place ourselves and our death-dealing voices at the foot of Christ's healing cross. The only thing we can do there is let ourselves be loved back to life. That's love's mysterious power, isn't it?

When we get serious about learning to be alive in God, we then start running into images of God that no longer fit with the God we are experiencing. It's only when we are able in grace to experience ourselves as God's beloved that these other voices are silenced—at least for a time. What are some current images you have of God that may be blocking out the true voice of your experience today? Do you still have images of God that no longer fit your experience of God today? Are there new images emerging in you by grace?

In 2012, at the same time that Americans by the millions slipped into a collective fright that Twinkies, Ding Dongs, and squiggle-topped cupcakes might go the way of the Pontiac, a significant celebration in the Vatican was relegated to the back pages of newspapers and thirty-second sound bites on broadcast news.

Michelangelo had finished the ceiling frescoes in the Sistine Chapel exactly five hundred years earlier, and the anniversary gave the whole world an opportunity to look at them again with fresh eyes, still amazed at their arresting beauty and their continuing power to evoke new and unexpected images of the relationship between God and the human family.

I visited the Sistine Chapel before its artistic restoration in the 1990s, when encrusted smoke and exhaust still held the colors of the frescoes captive. You may have seen before and after pictures of them or visited the chapel since the frescoes were cleaned. If so, you've seen the dazzling, resurrected colors that lurked too long beneath the grime. Not a bad image, actually, for what can happen with us if we allow God to do miraculous improvements and restorations in our lives.

While *lectio divina*, the practice of sacred reading, is a time-honored way of praying with Scripture, *visio divina*, sacred seeing, involves praying with works of art. We usually think of prayer as something we do in words, but if we change our perspective slightly, prayer might also be seen as God's wordless way of working in our hearts and lives. We hope to find our way into God's presence with the help of a chosen prayer practice.

Whether we pray by reading or seeing, the center of gravity in our prayer changes over time. After we've spent enough time with God's Word or an evocative piece of art, sooner or later we run out of thoughts and things to say. Only then does our interpretation stop, and God finally gets an opportunity to interpret our lives though Word and art in a way that is so arresting and beautiful, our lives will never again be the same.

You might consider leafing through pictures of the Sistine Chapel frescoes as a way of praying. I did it myself recently, and although I had casually looked at the frescoes hundreds of times before, I had never really seen them. When I looked at Michelangelo's depiction of the creation, my eyes were drawn to the space between the fingers of God and Adam. If I had done the fresco, the fingers would certainly have touched, probably my way of making sure everybody got the idea of life passing from God to Adam.

That alone proves why I'm no Michelangelo, since practicality and literalism often cannibalize indirection and image. The more time I spent with the fresco, the more I slowly realized that Michelangelo's genius had silently, ever so intimately captured the entire story of our relationship with God in that small, suggestive space between the fingers.

Isn't God always reaching out to us with new and eternal life? Our reaching out to God in response, however, is often less sure-footed and faithful. Instead, our lives are eternally suspended in that space between God's fingers and our own, between wounds that are never fully healed and grace never fully lived. Rather than finding life in that space of risk and hope, we pretend the fingers touch to soften the occasionally harsh ambiguity of spiritual growth.

I understand the theory of authentic growth, but something in me is still on the lookout for a divine sleight of hand that will absolve me from responsibility for the messy work of spiritual growth. Despite my supposed sophistication, I often still wish for a God who peddles cheap grace and reduces the cost of spiritual growth for final clearance.

I don't know about you, but it's taken me a long time to see that we have no huckster God. When I look for magic, God shows an infinitely patient sense of humor by gently knocking on my heart and inviting me to let God restore the grace hidden underneath. This is when God sees us, with Jesus, as "my beloved."

God, it seems, often believes in our beloved selves more strongly than we do, but no matter how many times we go kicking and screaming into God's remedial course on trust, we happily breathe a sigh of relief when we discover that God always grades on the curve.

In that luminous space between fingers—between our wounds and our healing—God keeps reaching out to us with abundant gifts of transforming love. It's only when we trust that love enough that the scales start to fall from our blinded eyes, and we see for ourselves how hard God works to reach out to us time and time again in comforting love. This is also the only sure path to spiritual growth: Be careful not to settle for anything less.

Life gets turned upside down on biblical mountaintops. Moses probably didn't think he'd be trudging down Mount Sinai carrying newly minted commandments etched into heavy stone tablets. Similarly, Peter, James, John, and even Jesus were awestruck when God's glory transfigured Jesus and everything looked, if only for a second, as bright as the sun. Maybe that's how sacraments got started: when divine life unexpectedly yet gracefully showed forth in the transfiguration of the ordinary.

One of my friends is a CPA with a big heart, a passion for helping disadvantaged kids, and an accountant's brain that thrives on clarity and order. He once asked me to define prayer. "OK," I said, "prayer is faith," to which he immediately shot back, "What does that mean?" "Think about it," I suggested, "and let's talk about it some more the next time we meet."

Faith is not prayer, but prayer is one of the activities of faith: taking time to intentionally look for God at work in our life calling us to more faithful commitment. As I sat in Starbucks on a Sunday afternoon, I was coming up empty trying to think of what to tell my friend the next time we talked.

Starbucks is, of course, not a mountaintop, but I've had to slowly learn to adjust my expectations when it comes to divine action in life. As I took a sip of my dark roast and looked to my left, I stumbled onto a stunning transfiguration that showed me what to say to him.

A thirty-something father in jeans and construction boots with a weekend's worth of stubble was sitting with his daughter and son at the table right next to me. His daughter was about three years old, and his son looked just this side of five. While she held a magic wand in one hand and wore a plastic tiara on her head, the boy was dressed like his dad, without the stubble but with the addition of a Minnesota Twins hoodie.

The place was packed and noisy, but the three of them seemed an island of radiant, silent intimacy right in the middle of all the chatter and hustle. The father was reading them a story, and the kids were transfixed by what they heard. They held their breath and their eyes were wide, clearly captivated by the story. While adults often struggle to be present or in the moment, these two were just being kids, practicing a way of paying attention we often have to relearn as adults. They were living inside the story, and their hearts burned as their dad's words read the story into their lives.

I sensed right away that what I had just seen lacked an accountant's need for literal precision, but I knew I had been given a momentary glance into the heart of prayer that my big-hearted accountant friend would get right away. After all, don't we often pray by just sitting comfortably while God speaks a saving story into our needy hearts? God's stories have the power to bring order to our chaos, hope to our despair, love to our restless hearts, and silence to our constant chatter.

Jesus worked tiny verbal miracles when he spoke parables into the lives of those who had ears to hear and eyes to see. Did you ever notice that the parables are all secular rather than overtly religious? They're just stories about ordinary human events in which, if we pay attention, we see ordinary stuff drenched in grace and silently looking out at us. In the end, God's stories aren't read: They happen.

It might sound irredeemably counterintuitive, but learning to pray sometimes means we stop saying prayers. If we stop talking for just a split second when we pray, maybe God will have a chance to get a word in edgewise. Like the two kids with their father, sometimes we just need to let God speak saving stories—some that comfort and others that challenge—into the tentative narrative of our lives.

So how do we learn to pray like this? Practice. The next time you prayerfully read a Scripture story, imagine that God is speaking it directly into your heart and life. If we take the kids listening to their father read them a story as a model, we allow ourselves to be drawn into the story's heart where small transfigurations can happen.

Take the time you need to listen to what comes to you during that prayer. Do it a number of times each week, and write down quick notes about how God seems to be at work in your prayer and in your life. Pay attention to the patterns that emerge over time. That's how our story and God's story become one story—the kind of story that can change and transfigure.

Can you remember a sermon about the Trinity that set your heart on fire? How about one on the theological virtues? Remember them? (Faith, hope, and love.) If you answered yes to either of these questions, consider yourself lucky, even blessed. If not, don't worry. You've got lots of company. For some inexplicable reason, Christians seems determined to make the living heart of our religious life — the Trinity and the theological virtues — sound lifeless, sterile, and abstract. How can living and loving seem so utterly boring?

Many Christians think of the Trinity as a thing, a mystery we just need to believe. And faith, hope, and love are things we have. Traditional theological language about the Trinity can also confuse and confound us. It's easy to imagine the Trinity as a baffling unity of three separate but equal divine Persons existing somewhere out there beyond space and time.

Bear with me as I use the male language of traditional Trinitarian theology. Karl Rahner, certainly one of the giants of twentieth-century Catholic theology, thought many Christians are trithe-ists rather than monotheists. In other words, they believe in three gods — Father, Son, and Holy Spirit — rather than in the one God of Christianity. After all, in the Creed we profess our belief in "one God, the Father."

Think of the Persons of the Trinity the same way we ordinarily think of a person — an individual center of consciousness capable of self-reflection and self-determination—and we'll eventually be sucked into a logical black hole. It also shows that popular conceptions of the Trinity as a community might be built on a foundation of theological quicksand.

Here's one more mystery about the Holy Mystery. Study theology and you can take courses in Christology (the study of the Son) and in pneumatology (the study of the Holy Spirit). You can study about God and the Trinity but, search as you may, you'll never find a course in Fatherology. So what do we know about our "one God, the Father"? And, really, what difference does it make? Stated simply, it makes all the difference.

What we know of God the Father is a summary of what we learn from Jesus in the Holy Spirit. This gives God a human face, and we get a hint of the intimacy Jesus felt with God when he used images of parenthood, origin, future, and sustenance to describe it. We're offered the same kind of intimacy, and this means that, as Christians, we're invited to find our life in the Trinity of God. Rather than being way out there somewhere, we find the Trinity at work right here among us—creating, saving, loving, and forgiving us into spiritual growth.

One of my theology professors, Leo J. O'Donovan, S.J., once suggested that we think of the persons of the Trinity as settings or situations of God rather than as people. Momentarily set aside the "what" questions and focus instead on "where" and "how" questions, and we might catch a fresh glimpse of how God lives with us. In what kind of settings might we stumble into God?

The best place to look is into the humanity we share with Jesus. It's there that God has chosen to live, and God's own Holy Spirit gives us the creative courage to take a chance on the God of Jesus as the authentic source and future of our lives. In other words, we reach from and toward God when we respond to God's gracious offer of life in faith, hope, and love. Live in these virtues, and God shows us deeply and clearly the eternal significance of our lives, the lives of our neighbors, and the life of our world.

Jesus saw God alive and at work when healing, love, challenge, and forgiveness happened. As God came to life in these kinds of situations, our humanity is transfigured into God's environment, the place in which God has chosen to live with you and me. Only there do God's life and ours get wrapped up in the glory of grace.

Staking our lives on the God of Jesus means that despite the hate, brutality, and injustice in our world, we still profess a sober and unromantic belief that the final word of it all is eternally sheltering, creative, loving, sustaining. This is the source of the compassionate hope that undergirds our efforts for love and justice.

Our true life with God is allowing God to draw us into divine life, and for us to invite God into ours. Think of this as the activity of prayer and service. When we look into our hearts and the eyes of our neighbor, God's inviting presence seems so stunningly simple and beautiful that our faith is stripped of pretense and abstraction. Words like *setting* and *situation* feel flat, without texture, devoid of depth. Silent adoration and self-forgetting service is our own true response before our "One God, the Father."

I was once involved in a Sunday evening Eucharist for an intentional community in Detroit. Every Sunday, just like clockwork, the same guy showed up five minutes before Mass and asked the same priest to hear his confession. The priest was a friend of mine, so I finally asked him why this man needed the sacrament of reconciliation every week without exception. Without missing a beat, the priest told me that, "He wants to be forgiven for being alive."

Granted, this obviously represents one jaw-dropping extreme, but as a spiritual director, I'm often taken aback by the harsh accusatory tone in the language we sometimes use about ourselves. It seems as though we're forever telling ourselves that, "I never," or "I must," or "I have to," or "I ought." If we really listen to these memos to self, we might start to hear a self-derisive voice under it all telling us that even God—or anybody else, for that matter—couldn't love us the way we really are.

What kind of image of God and self leads to such harsh self-appraisals? Exposing these unforgiving images to the healing gaze of God's uncompromising compassion is often the first step in real spiritual growth.

On the other hand, there are people who have little sense of sin at all. Anything they do that even slightly smacks of moral culpability is charged off as an imperfection rather than a sin, the product of upbringing and culture rather than personal choice. Bring up the subject of sin today and then prepare yourself for wide-ranging reactions, from utter indifference to white-hot passion and even anger.

Our involvement with sin ranges from over-involvement—think of the first gentleman I referenced—to under-involvement, like the other people I described. In other words, some of us see ourselves teeming with sin, while others have little sense of sin at all. Don't you agree that there has to be a middle course in which culpability is appropriately experienced without self-loathing and chronic, paralyzing guilt and shame?

In *Speaking Christian*, Protestant theologian Marcus Borg suggests that the word *sinner* has emerged in Christian history as the fundamental metaphor of our relationship with God. Yet imagining our relationship with God as primarily avoiding sin so we don't offend God and risk being punished for our wrongdoing is a monstrously restrictive way to live and believe.

It seems an equally unbalanced view, as irresponsible as it is sad, to refuse to believe that we are capable of evil and sin. Granted that we are all the victims of the deeply engrained, unrecognized effects of faulty personal and religious formation or socially enshrined strictures of control and oppression, we all have to face the harsh reality that each of us can freely and deliberately choose to do or cooperate with evil.

These two extremes are overdrawn caricatures, with elements of truth and falsity in both, but we don't live as caricatures in this kind of either/or world with an either/or God, risking over-involvement or under-involvement at every turn. If we feel pulled in this direction, it's a sign we need to spend healing time with our both/and God. God, it seems, has a lot more patience seeing us with balanced vision as loved sinners than we do. As we ponder our dark side with the Lord, we learn to enjoy our grace and repent our sin.

There's another side of sin we don't think about often. Most of the time, we think of the sins we commit, while failing to see sinful situations in and around us from which individual sins arise. To finally come to a balanced sense of our sinful selves, however, we also have to take seriously how we've been sinned against, rather than only concentrating on what we do. Not only have we done evil to others, but others have also done real damage to us. Who are they? How have they hurt us? How does this sin against us still play out in our lives? How might we possibly forgive them and in the process learn to forgive ourselves in the infinite, merciful forgiveness that comes to us in Jesus?

In taking appropriate responsibility for our sinful selves and for acting against the chronic overtones of sin we still experience because of the sins of others, our gift is often the spiritual binocularity we looked at earlier. Our sense of sin and grace are concrete instances of how healing such a view can be for us.

Once again, our sense of self as sinner and saint at the same time is possible only because God has opened our eyes to see how they finally meet on the horizon of the Holy Mystery. The words of Jesus always call us to cast off our sin, but, in the process, we're never condemned—only called.

Let's create an imaginary spreadsheet with two columns. Mark the first "positive" and the second "negative." We'll fill in each column with five examples of offhanded comments others have made to us that have stuck—for good or ill, for a time or even a lifetime.

This idea stemmed from a lunch I had with Ken, a friend and somebody I once coached in an executive leadership program. Somewhere in the middle of our burgers and fries, he told me he only remembers one thing I ever told him. (It had to be one of my brilliant insights about strategic leadership, I figured, but I couldn't have been more wrong.) "One day," he said, "when you were leaving, you looked at me and said, 'Trust your instincts. They're pretty good.' That comment," he concluded, "helped me a lot."

That got me thinking about offhanded comments I've received that still influence me today. The people who made them probably don't remember making them, but for some reason, they've stuck with me.

The next morning I headed to Starbucks with journal in hand, ready to make my spreadsheet come alive with real examples, both positive and negative. I know you have your own, but let me share a few just to get you thinking.

When I was in my early thirties, somebody casually told me that my sense of humor would be my salvation. It sounded interesting in a non-earthshaking way, but it's proved prophetic. When my world turns dark, I can usually find a trace of (black) humor in it, and that's what gives me enough detachment from the darkness that I don't lose myself in it. That way, it turns out to be part of my life, not all of it.

A wise retreat director once stopped me in mid-sentence and told me to stop babbling. "It feels like you're bringing me geometry homework to correct," she said, impatiently. "Where's your heart in all this?" Ever since then, searching for my heart has become a daily activity.

I heard the same thing when I did the thirty-day version of the Spiritual Exercises for the second time. The only thing that sticks after a month's worth of conversations with my director was when he asked me if understanding things was enough for me. Some themes in our lives never change, they just give us ongoing opportunities to keep begging Jesus for healing. But we can all also cite negative examples, can't we?

I once took at course from a Zen teacher who talked so slowly that I had to bite my tongue so I didn't finish her sentences for her. But one night she asked two questions that stopped us all in our tracks.

"How many of you," she asked, "remember a physical injury you suffered as a child that still affects you today?" One or two hands went up. "How many of you," she went on, "remember a hurtful comment you received as a child that still affects you?" Every hand went up.

For example, I know my mother loved me, but that never stopped her from looking for opportunities to improve me. Unfortunately, however good her intentions, such efforts were wasted on me as a kid. It always felt like she was never satisfied with how I was, and that hurt a lot.

I visited her once when I was an adult, and she told me about all the strange stuff I used to say as a kid. "You would look at me and say, 'Don't talk hard at me, Mommy.'" She thought it was funny, but I heard it with an adult brain still inside the skin of the kid I always felt like with her. Right then I understood clearly why I spent so much of my life expecting to be screamed at by authority figures.

The organizer of our eighth-grade party forgot to invite me, but when I innocently asked her about it, she just said, "Oh, you're not invited." That's the kind of comment that excommunicates a fourteen–year-old from life. These are the kinds of words that really do take on flesh and affect how we see ourselves, others, and even God.

I put my journal down, realizing for the first time that memory plays everything back in stereo. One channel plays only the good stuff—the golden oldies—while the other plays only tales from the dark side. We can't stop either channel from playing but, as adults, we can decide which one will dominate.

Allowed to play at full volume, negative comments can bring us down, but prayer can help us turn down the volume on our internal bully and accuser. Their shrill, destructive voices need not dominate. Only then can we hear the loving voice that arises out of silence: "You are my beloved. I delight in you." That's a message that needs to be written in our heart's journal every day.

Finding refuge from a desert filled with dangers in a safe, well-protected city filled with people of peace is one of the deep desires embedded in the psalms. It's also a deep desire for many of us today. Aren't we also looking for a place where we'll find others intent on living close to the heart of grace and growth? We need to keep our eyes wide open as we look, however, because communities of faith can pop up where we least expect them.

Even though I've written pious thoughts about our need for silence, I actually work best surrounded by hustle, music, and conversation — my own brand of white noise. That's why Starbucks has become my rent-free office. Spending time there has also sharpened my powers of observation, and what I've learned is that Starbucks has become a new gathering place for spiritual seekers.

People in recovery — from teenager to golden-ager — pack my Starbucks and have tough, bone-honest, and spiritually charged conversations. Challenge equals caring for them, and sanity lurks at the intersection of desire, addiction, and literal delivery from death. Death and resurrection couldn't be more real.

Most Sundays a Hmong kid curls up in an easy chair, Joel Osteen in hand, while a woman sits opposite him lost in Dietrich Bonheoffer. Bible readers are also there every day, and they systematically attack their texts with yellow, pink, and green highlighters, each color, I'm sure, signifying a different layer of meaning. Weekday regulars include a talkative, fidgety guy who, when not talking with cops on their breaks, fights to keep his eyes open and his head buried in a book called *The Dynamic Laws of Prayer*.

Thich Nhat Hanh is a favorite author among regulars, as are an apparently infinite number of books by and about Thomas Merton. *The Power of Now* by Eckhart Tolle, however, is the hands-down favorite, and *Now* groups and Bible groups regularly compete for premium space.

Today's enlightened churches actively foster spiritual growth, but some still just talk about God with too little attention paid to our instinctive hunger to experience God. Ignatius Loyola got it right back in the sixteenth century when he commented that, "It is not in an abundance of knowledge that the soul is satisfied, but with the interior sense and taste of spiritual things." It's this interior knowledge that people want, and they'll shop around until they find people and communities to support their quest.

Disillusionment with organized religion or inexperience with anything traditionally religious lands many at Starbucks. A sizeable number of people I see for spiritual direction are actively church shopping or looking for credible reasons to stick with their religious communities of origin. Until our ecclesial communities do a better job of initiating people into the experience of the Holy Mystery that gives religion life, people will keep trying to go it alone or find communities of their own. Eventually, many of them wind up at Starbucks.

I've often borrowed a wonderful image from *Stopping*, a book by David Kuntz. He asks readers to imagine a tree and then draw it. Whenever I've used this exercise, everybody without exception draws only half the tree, the part above ground. But there's another half below ground we can't see, and it's from there that a tree draws much of its strength and flexibility.

Too often we also fall into the same limiting perspective. I can't speak for others, but I often put too much faith in what is above ground: money, clothes, cars, and a wide variety of electronic gadgets. Churches can also invest too heavily above ground—regulations, disembodied dogma and theology, even matching vestments and parking lot repairs.

In the end the tree is whole, and although we construct mental distinctions between what's above and below ground, they overlap in real life. As a result, we need to carve out careers just as churches need to repair parking lots while also searching below ground for the spark of the Spirit. Dualities in our personal and communal lives—above and below, flesh and spirit, nature and grace, dogma and mysticism—finally dissolve in the utter unity and simplicity of God's call to become one in the life of grace.

It's sometimes an abrupt change in perspective when we finally see and understand that God doesn't speak in doctrinal proposition. God speaks first as the creative mystery that is our origin, life, and future. Without a home in Holy Mystery, dogma is rendered sterile and faith risks being uninspiring and uninformed.

Maybe my Starbucks is unique, but take a close look inside your own and you'll see traces of what I've described here. Unless more of our ecclesial homes become gathering places for those who want the interior sense and taste of spiritual things, we might have to start putting steeples on Starbucks stores.

PART TWO

SO

WHAT?

Dilemmas

of

Discipleship

When photographer Robert Mapplethorpe died of AIDS in 1989, he left a body of work that was as brilliant as it was controversial. Many of his photographs were unapologetically charged with homoerotic themes that shocked and even disgusted many people. His work was enthusiastically admired by some, thoughtfully criticized by others, and ignorantly savaged by many.

Mapplethorpe claimed his imagination was deeply formed by the traditional Catholicism of his childhood, and he thought of each of his photographs as an altar, a sacred space for giving back to God. His artistic impulse, he believed, resulted from "holding hands with God," and his ambition was to look at the world with fresh, bold eyes, seeing what nobody else had ever seen before in people, sexuality, and even violence.

Just about the time he died, I bought a print of one of a series of portraits Mapplethorpe made of Tim Scott, a model he often used. Pencil thin with a tattooed right arm, he looked straight ahead, left hand raised in front of his spiked hair to shield his eyes from the glare. One reason I bought the print was to prove I was suitably edgy in my tastes, but something deeper in the portrait also attracted me, although it was twenty years before I saw it as an invitation to step into the reign of God.

Tim Scott's portrait shares my living room wall with Emerson Burkhart's self-portrait, a painting I described earlier as a persistent image of God for me. While I see God as presence in Burkhart's painting, Mapplethorpe's portrait shows me God at work, always scanning the horizon, looking for opportunities to invite us to deeper life and keep us safe from harm. He's a younger version of the prodigal son's father in Luke's Gospel (chapter fifteen), someone on the lookout for his lost son, to welcome him home at long last.

We also catch a glimpse of the Christian at work in the portrait. Being in God's presence and held in love, sin and all, is never enough for us. The love given us by Jesus compels us to also keep our eyes peeled for opportunities to love and serve. Despite our perennial temptation to turn God into an abstraction, God prefers incarnation and loves coming alive eternally in human flesh and blood. Receiving love and freely giving it away only to be given it again is the mystery of our life in God, a life that finds completion in ever more faithful discipleship.

Discipleship—the humble service of love for the sake of God over time—is born in our vocations, commitments, and decisions. The parent who gets up early every morning to feed the kids and get them off to school is every bit as much a disciple as the Trappist monk who gets up and prays with his brothers every day at three o'clock in the morning. We also see discipleship at work in the person who has called the person they love every afternoon for the past forty years just to see how things are going and say, "I love you." And there's the priest who could get by reading canned homilies, but chooses instead to take the time he needs to find something personally significant to share every day at Mass.

There's also the substance abuse counselor who's seen the same person fall off the wagon time after time and never loses faith in their inherent human dignity as one of God's beloved. What about the politician who endures personal criticism but does the right thing, or the corporate executive who feels compelled by faith to honor promises and tell the truth? These ways of being selfless come from a heart that knows God's fidelity personally and shares it naturally, simply, graciously.

The practical discernment needed to live as a disciple of Jesus requires that we also protect our hearts from the glaring temptations of pride, self-derision, complacency, or cynicism. You and I are also called to look steadily into the heart of the world and see God almost undetectably at work there, offering life, forgiveness, hope, and courage. Our love and service turns out to be our own altar, a sacred place where divine love and human love find ways to overlap and get mixed in together.

Discipleship often comes down to the concrete, daily decisions we make about how we choose to love others and ourselves for God's sake. It's usually nothing at all flashy, just showing up prepared to love. Take the time you need to remember and thank people who over time have proved themselves disciples of Jesus to you. But don't stop there. Be sure to remember and give thanks for the gifts you've received. This is how we hold hands with God, and God with us.

Admiration, attraction, and ambition are interrelated moments in Christian discipleship. They may not be the kinds of words we usually associate with discipleship, but they just might let us look at it with fresh eyes.

Think of three people you admire for who they are, what they stand for, and how they've influenced you. What is it about them that holds your attention? Perhaps it's their personal mystery: There's just something about them we find admirable and attractive.

That "just something" quality is central. Not only are we attracted to people we admire, we also want to be with them, get to know them, and get inside their vision. For example, I admire my dad for his quiet, unshakable love for his family and the people he served in his medical practice. He took care of people who couldn't pay, treated migrant workers when nobody else would, and sometimes delivered two babies before going to work the next morning.

I'd like to live like my dad, and I regret I never got to know him better. But as an adult, I figure I get to know him better as I know myself better. He was that kind of powerful, mysterious force in my life.

Ambition turns out to be the disciple's capstone virtue. It's typically associated with pride and a ruthless winner-take-all, get-them-before-they-get-me grab for money, power, and ego satisfaction. This kind of ambition is blind, because it's indifferent to anyone or anything that doesn't help it achieve its goals. Think greed, manipulation, duplicity. Think Wall Street in recent years.

But that's not the only kind of ambition. There's an equally determined kind of ambition that has had its ego tamed enough to transform the energy of self-seeking into a drive for service. Think about the relentless ambition of the apostle Paul to take the Gospel to the ends of the earth, or what was required by the disciples to act on the command of Jesus to make disciples of all nations. The demands of the Gospel require more than an occasional, stingy nod to pretend selflessness. Ambition is required to do great deeds for God and God's people, and it's the Gospel that gives birth to holy ambition.

The root of the word *ambition* means to be filled with awe and wonder at something we see. What was it about my dad that filled me with awe and a desire to be like him? And what is it about the person and mission of Jesus that still inspires admiration for his vision of the reign of God and a desire to be with him in discipleship?

What draws you in as you read the Gospels, struggle to pray, and spend time with companions of Jesus? The grace we are given as we come to know Jesus more intimately and follow him more intentionally is born in admiration and attraction. There's just something about him that also awakens a holy ambition in us to be with Christ in his ministry of healing and reconciliation.

The Gospels give us privileged glimpses of Jesus in love, at prayer, and at work. And as we get deeper and more realistic glimpses of our world, we hope to be filled with the desire to do our part to heal its wounds. Discipleship is finally just falling in love with the God of Jesus in the power of the Holy Spirit. It's the Holy Spirit, after all, that lights the fires of holy ambition.

All this talk about ambition—holy or not—can discourage us as much as it can build us up. We can be tempted to think that Christianity is only meant for saints, and certainly not for the likes of you and me. If you find yourself feeling that way, consider it a temptation. It's certainly not a grace.

Holy ambition can lead a person to take leadership in projects to promote peace, ensure justice, clothe the naked, and welcome the stranger. It also requires a kind of holy ambition, doesn't it, to do the day-to-day interior work that's part of spiritual growth. Holy ambition calls us to get involved in the deeds of love, service, and justice that are needed in the day-to-day world in which we live.

What attracts you to people you admire? Your response may help you identify their mysterious "just something" quality. What might this suggest about you and them? Take time to write about your relationship to these folks. Don't settle for generalizations, but identify exactly what it is about them that draws you to them. Don't just think—write. It requires commitment, and what we write can keep us focused and accountable over time.

Ten Thousand Villages is a retail chain with a store in St. Paul. It's a curious place, stocked with items from developing countries. I visited it about a decade ago and, for some inexplicable reason, walked out with a bag of polished stones with words engraved on them. One said *love*, another *strength*, and still another *wisdom*. Rounding out the set were other stones with *joy*, *hope*, and *creativity* etched on them.

Since I have a built-in disdain for anything that smacks of New Age hokum, I couldn't explain my attraction to these stones, but buy them I did and, even more remarkably, I took them with me when I moved to Dallas and brought them with me when I moved back to Minnesota. They've all found a home on the coffee table in my living room, and I paid little attention to them until recently.

The coffee table where they rest is right in front of me when I try to pray, and—as strange as it sounds—I'm convinced they started staring at me a couple months ago. I retaliated by staring back, and upped the ante in our staring contest when I placed a rough stone I found outside among its more sophisticated, polished cousins.

As we learn to pray and eventually let God pray in us, we're usually led into the heart of our deepest desires. I don't know about you, but the initial challenge in this process is learning the difference between thinking about what we want and learning about what we really need, the bedrock of our deepest desires.

It's only when God pushed me in this direction, when I took a chance and stepped into the person of Bartimaeus, learning to shout out my needs to Jesus (see Mark 10:47), that my stone collection turned into a significant ally in my prayer.

Instinctively it seems, I started reaching out during prayer for the stone that most closely named what I desired and needed from God. Reaching out, picking up, and holding a stone gradually became a common prayer practice for me. Doing so was probably God's way of getting prayer out of its customary home in my head and reaching into my real needs and desires symbolized in an equally tangible way in the stones.

I'd reach for *creativity* one day and for *peace* the next, doing something to express the needs I really felt. I particularly remember grabbing stones when I was praying early one Sunday morning. My prayer that day was filled with distractions and interior chatter, so I reached for the stone marked *strength* and held it tightly. After a couple of minutes, however, I realized that I had picked up the wrong stone.

Call it grace or intuition, but it finally occurred to me that *strength* was the last thing I needed. After all, I usually have more strength and muscle than I know what to do with and, if I'm not careful, I'll try to muscle my way through prayer and life.

So I put it back and reached for the stone marked *love*, finally seeing that I simply needed to be loved for a change. Luckily, God is in the love business, and there's plenty for us all if we just ask for it. I also learned that day that I might not always be the best judge of what I need.

In spiritual direction, I often meet people who are in the same space. I gradually started suggesting to people that they might find it helpful to do the same thing when we talked to make sure our conversation is kept grounded in what is unmistakably real. It's proved to be an exercise that is as comforting as it is clarifying.

The rough alley stone gradually became the desire still looking for a name. It also came to feel like the stones the accusers finally had to drop rather than throw after Jesus confronted them in John's story of the woman caught in adultery. Even more to the point, that rough stone started to stand for all the stones I'd learned to throw at myself when shame and despair held my heart captive. In other words, it's how I'm tempted to treat myself when, due to my occasionally impaired spiritual binocularity, I can only see what's wrong with me.

This is what can happen when we lose sight of living in the light of God's loving gaze or if we fail to take our place with Bartimaeus in making our real needs known. Naming what we really need and reaching out for it is grace in action. I'm sure you'd agree with me that trying to go it alone and relying on our own pride-filled strength is too tiring and lonely.

Remember the last time you had one of those days, when you've had it up to your ears with everybody who wants something from you? "Attention everyone," you think, "don't even think about asking me to do one more thing." That's when we know the phone will ring or somebody will knock at the door. At that point, even a simple request feels intrusive.

I think Jesus felt that way too, sometimes. For example, read the story of the cure of the Canaanite woman's daughter (Matthew 15:21–28). Jesus seemed sick to death of arguing with religious authorities and taking care of all the others who wanted something from him. That's why he "withdraws," probably just like us, to be by himself for a chance to regain perspective. It's a clear case of compassion fatigue.

Just when Jesus thinks he's found a temporary retreat, a Canaanite woman finds out where he is and screams at him to heal her daughter. The disciples agree with her and plead with him to give her what she wants.

Not only is Jesus unmoved by their request, but, since the woman is a gentile, he insists that his ministry is only for Jews. But she won't take no for an answer and reminds Jesus that even dogs eat the scraps that fall from their master's table. Jesus finally comes to his senses, sees that he's in the presence of great faith—even in a gentile—and grants her request.

But hold on, I thought Jesus was perfect. How could he get irked with people? Isn't that wrong? Wasn't he always running after people to help them? Wasn't he the one who just gave and gave and never paid attention to his own needs? Needs? Did Jesus really have needs? What if Jesus wasn't what we'd call perfect?

The words *Jesus* and *perfect* are so intimately connected in the Christian imagination that I wonder if we ever think about what we mean when we say them. Are we just pretending to understand when we read that Jesus was like us in all things but sin (Hebrews 4:15)? Christians readily admit that Jesus probably had to learn things, but did he have to get over prejudices and misunderstandings just like the rest of us?

What if he occasionally made personal blunders and messed up relationships just like the rest of us? His interaction with the Canaanite woman might give us a hint.

Since Matthew's Gospel was written for a Jewish audience, Scripture scholars often link this story to the argument in the early Church about whether the reign of God Jesus proclaimed extended even to faith-filled gentiles. What if we read this story from the viewpoint that even Jesus could be proved wrong, and finally had to give up his attachment to his own religious and cultural prejudices? When does a godly perfectionism eclipse the possibility of personal growth? In other words, whom do we allow to be our teacher?

In Matthew's story, Jesus finally and even begrudgingly let the Canaanite woman teach him that his world was too small. Apparently, the reign of God has a zero-tolerance policy for exclusion. I know I have a hard time with this policy, and, although I hate to admit it, at times so does my Church.

43

Do you remember ever having to swallow your pride and learn an important lesson from somebody you disliked or even despised? If you do, you probably know what it feels like for the reign of God to take hold. But sometimes the reign of God shows up when we are also spiritually free enough to stand our ground. Knowing the difference is the business of discernment. All I know is that prejudice usually comes with a scream, but love most often comes with a whisper, a compassionate nod, even silence.

Look at this question socially, and you'll have to decide who counts and who doesn't, who speaks with the authority of God and who doesn't. Can all of us—churches included—be changed by the poor, the disabled, immigrants, and other marginalized people? Can we accept these and others into our lives and churches as equals rather than guests? Are we prepared as well to learn from what the Gospels have to say about business and the economy, violence and war?

Our faith, hope, and love are always a work in progress. It looks like this is something we share with Jesus.

| THE ODOR OF SIN |

A wise Church invites us to rub up against our permanent need for repentance and forgiveness each year during the six weeks of Lent. Six weeks is a long time and, if we aren't careful, we might conclude that the Church is preoccupied with sin and the passion and death of Jesus.

But that would be a mistake. The Church also celebrates our resurrected life with Jesus for an equally long time during the Easter season — actually, a week longer. Understanding this holy balancing act is one thing. Living it is another.

Let's start with sin. Have you ever felt an embarrassing, humiliating, and even visceral need to repent and get past the guilt sin brings? It happened to me on Ash Wednesday a couple years ago. With fresh, gritty ashes on my forehead, grace and common sense colluded to convince me that I needed to give things up during Lent that year. Both also urged me to get out of the stands and into the game so God could rough me up just enough to get the spotlight off of me and fixed on Jesus.

A story still circulates about a group of young Jesuit seminarians, dutifully lined up to go to confession. Supposedly they all looked down at the floor when they heard the elderly priest confessor bellow at his current penitent, "Imperfection nothing, that's a mortal sin!" When the red-faced seminarian came out of the confessional, everybody pretended they hadn't heard a thing. They knew they could be next.

My face got rubbed in my supposed imperfections a few times just before Ash Wednesday that year, the first starting in my car on a cold Sunday morning. Parked outside the Quaker Meeting House I visit occasionally, I saw a woman hauling boxes of cookies and containers of coffee into the building. She needed help, and, as I slouched down in my seat, I made the decision: "I'm not going to help you."

After she disappeared inside, I slipped in, waiting impatiently for cookies and coffee while I also waited for God to give me that holy feeling. I rationalized what I did by telling myself that I was always too quick to take care of other people's needs, but I knew in that deep-down, self-evident way that I had decided to be downright selfish. I had sinned.

Fast-forward a couple weeks, when I stopped for coffee before heading to the airport. After I grabbed my dark roast and sat down, in walked a street person whose stench preceded him. He got coffee and looked for a seat while I looked at him and thought, "Don't come near me."

Luckily he plopped into a leather chair near the door, while I breathed more easily and whispered to myself, "Thank God you're over there. I don't want anything to do with you." He probably didn't want anything to do with me either, but pride often spills over into the grandiose lie that the world revolves around us.

Thinking about him led me to think about the Quaker woman, and by the time I reached the airport, conscience took a jackhammer to my blacktopped heart and exposed the festering self-indulgence that had been hidden for so long. As I boarded the plane I thought, "That guy holds a privileged place in God's kingdom. So does the coffee and cookie lady." I knew in my heart I wouldn't be getting a kingdom invitation that year.

Right then I smelled another nasty odor, but this time it came from the stench of my smug, arrogant pride. My pretend imperfections took on the sure smell of sin again, and I wondered how many other viruses were harbored undetected in my heart, infecting my attitudes and behaviors.

By the time we landed, I felt embarrassed, guilty, and disgusted with myself. Maybe you've also noticed it; times like these come with a grace all their own. A sure sign of God's growing life in us is experiencing our sin without the isolating and debilitating guilt that can wind up turning us away from God.

It takes a long time for us to get over our chronic belief that we will never be quite good enough for God or anybody else to really love us. We don't have to scrub off our sin so God can love us. Instead, when we allow God's healing love to touch us, we want to leave sin behind. Growth starts in love, not in guilt. Our guilt doesn't go away, but it can slowly be transformed as we learn to live in the loving gaze of God.

Learning to say no to ourselves opens us to the possibility of seeking life outside ourselves. This kind of repentance never ends, but it starts only when we can see ourselves as God sees us: a loved sinner.

Executive recruiters joke that Minnesota is one of the hardest place to get people to move to, but once here, it's almost impossible to lure them away. There's something infectious about this place.

Moving to Minnesota and becoming a Minnesotan are not the same, and calling a new place home comes with unspoken yet mandatory rites of passage. After all, who doesn't hate the "you're not from around here" designation? To earn bragging rights as a real Minnesotan, you've got to brave sub-zero temperatures without losing your sense of humor, and you also have to visit the headwaters of the Mississippi River.

I've lived through plenty of bitterly cold winters here but only recently earned my headwaters merit badge. To do it I had to drag myself out of bed way too early one morning, scarf down some maple-flavored oatmeal, gas up the car, and head north out of St. Paul armed with a gigantic, environmentally hostile Styrofoam cup of convenience-store coffee.

Four hours later I parked at the north end of Lake Itasca in northern Minnesota, and in just minutes I was struggling to keep my balance as I walked across the rocks that mark where the lake ends and the river starts. The rocks were added when the river's source was widened, an "improvement" on nature made in the 1930s, but if you walk just a little upstream, you can actually step across the "Mighty Mississipp." For whatever reason, stepping across wasn't enough, so

I took off my shoes and socks and waded into the icy water for a few minutes, not quite sure why I felt compelled to get wet.

Later that day I drove east across Minnesota's Iron Range where I spent the night in Hibbing, Bob Dylan's hometown, passing Judy Garland's family home in Grand Rapids on my way back home the next morning. When I thought about my brief foray into the river, what I remembered most was that, even that close to its source, I could feel the river's current already pushing and pulling as it began its ninety-day trek to the Gulf of Mexico.

The more I thought about it, I came to see my stepping into the river as way of understanding the prayer practice called the examen more deeply. Catholics have always been encouraged to examine their consciences regularly, particularly before celebrating the sacrament of reconciliation. Unfortunately, this exercise typically focuses on only one dimension of our relationship with God—our sins—and for generations of Catholics, it perpetuated an equally one-sided image of God as heavenly judge.

Ignatius Loyola, however, suggested we do the examen as an examination of consciousness, or an awareness prayer. As a result, we were to understand all the influences—those that move us toward or away from God—on a regular basis.

For example, as I look back over my day, what currents moved me toward or away from a particular way of thinking or acting? Were they from God or were there also currents that originated in selfish or destructive sources? Distinguishing between good and evil is usually clear, but what about the currents we experience that only seem to be from God and will, in the end, lead us away from life and grace? As Scripture warns us, the enemies of God often dress up like angels of light. This is when the discernment of spirits comes into play. In other words, how do we see things for what they really are so we know which currents come from a place of life and goodness and, as a result, stand the best chance of leading us in that direction?

It's easy to hear all this talk about discernment and immediately conclude it's something that is ultimately too hard and complicated to be of much use to us as we strive to be faithful to God's call in our life. We can, however, take strength in realizing that any current we experience in ourselves that discourages and troubles us from following the Lord in faith, hope, and love can't be from God. Take Galatians 5:18–23 to heart: It's a good guide to what currents that come from God look like.

God can slowly teach us the sound of the divine voice, the feel of the divine current moving in our lives. Learning in God's grace to recognize and distinguish the variety of currents that can and do move us, and to choose those that lead us to be fully alive is what it means to do God's will. Doing God's will means to be fully alive in God.

Just as the Mississippi River's current eventually spills over into the Gulf of Mexico, God's powerful current in our lives will, we hope, carry us along into infinite, silent Holy Mystery of our God. It's only when we look back that we can see how God was always the real current in our lives all along.

We each have personal ways for mourning our losses and containing our grief. My parents had a good-natured argument throughout most of their married life about the coat on the banister. My dad always left his coat there, and mom always told him to hang it in the closet where it belonged, although both secretly knew nothing would ever change.

After dad's death, knowing full well he'd never hang his coat on the banister again, mom sometimes hung it on the banister as a momentary gesture to tame the savage loss she felt. Mourning takes time, and grief has its own timetable for healing.

Grief and mourning are constant companions in our spiritual lives. When we accept God's invitation to grow, we're forced to leave behind our accumulated substitutes for God. I used to think I knew a lot about mourning and grief, but it wasn't until I learned about the Leopard Queen that I really saw what loss was all about.

I log most of my TV time watching Animal Planet or National Geographic Wild. Documentaries about animals with fur, especially big cats like lions, cheetahs, and leopards, particularly draw me in, while stories about animals with scales, gills, feathers, or suction cups leave me cold. Big cats live directly and instinctively, certainly without the intellectual insulation we often bring to our experience.

One Saturday afternoon I stumbled onto a BBC documentary, *Leopard Queen*, that followed the life of a female leopard, Manana, from birth until she disappeared seventeen years later. Halfway through the film, she gave birth to a single cub, a new life that instinctively demanded her protection and care—her consummate attention. Leopards are great tree climbers, but until a cub learns this life-saving skill, the mother hides it when she heads out to hunt. Instinct locks the cub in place until the mother returns.

One day Manana returned to find her cub missing. Sensing her world had just been turned upside down, agitation overtook her as she set out, resolved to find it. She finally hunted down the snake that had swallowed the cub whole and heartlessly harassed it until it spit out the dead cub's remains and slithered away.

Manana picked up the dead cub, carried it back to her den, cleaned it, and then ate it. For the next week, she sat in a tree and called night and day for the cub she knew was dead. When she could call no longer, she walked away to find a new place to live.

Something in the bold simplicity of her ritual captivated me, probably her intense focus and instinctive connection with the deep down pulse of life and death. Her ritual was simple, and perhaps by reason of its simplicity, it was acutely resonant: panic, searching, finding, feeding, mourning, and moving on. My own mourning, I sensed, could stand more internalizing and less avoidance, less muted expression and more extroverted wailing against loss.

Perhaps we don't get hired for a job we wanted or our kids abruptly turn away from what we worked so hard to teach them, or our spouse or partner leaves us—forever. Maybe the Church in which we've found our home for so long feels polarized and combative. We each have our own examples, don't we, because none of us is exempt from the emptiness of losing something or someone we leaned on for strength.

The stuff of spiritual growth—wanting to love more selflessly, pray more simply, or serve more freely—calls us to put aside the subtle ways we are fixed in fear. Our graced challenge is to spend time to mourn what we've lost and gather the strength to look for ways of living closer to the pulse of God's life.

When we hit times like these, *visio divina* could be a fruitful way for us to pray. Just spending time looking at images of Michelangelo's gorgeous sculpture, the *Pieta*, might well be the only way we can really pray. In times of intense loss and grief, we take our place with Mary as she embraces all our grief in her own as she silently holding in her arms the stark presence of our suffering God in the lifeless body of her Son.

That's also what the Leopard Queen did instinctively when she lost her cub: She sat in the tree and cried out until her pain began to loosen its grip. Our faith grows only in the silent belief that we will not be abandoned to death without hope.

If you or someone you know suffers from depression, like me, you know it acts like a leak in a tire: It slowly yet ever so surely deflates the imagination until everything seems flat, lifeless, and colorless, leaving a person checkmated by an unforgiving, dark hopelessness. Without an ever-changing array of medications prescribed by a savvy psychiatrist, my own depression would soon—within days, I've learned—wrestle me to the ground.

I probably inherited my depression from my mom, who was also seriously depressed. A weighty sadness sometimes lurked in our home like a vampire ready to pounce and suck the life out of you. Mom's life might have proved more satisfying had she talked with somebody about how she felt or considered taking medication. But she was independent, stubborn, and willful, a well-practiced old-school Irish Catholic. And unfortunately, like mother, like son.

Mom bore her dark mood as a cross, maybe even God's will. However she looked at it, she put up with it with martyr-like resignation. I don't think she ever knew what happiness felt like and, given her history, happiness might have frightened her by reason of its unfamiliarity. If she had gotten as mad at her depression as she seemed at herself, her healing might have had a fighting chance.

Anyone committed to the hard work of spiritual growth knows it comes with ongoing joys, challenges, and critical discernments. I've learned from my own experience, and from that of others whom I've talked with in spiritual direction, that depression sometimes forces us to take an alternate route to wholeness, one that comes with twists and turns all its own. With enough practice, we can slowly learn to negotiate the distinctive geography depression can bring to the spiritual path.

God's job, I think, is to keep lovingly disrupting our lives, and our job is to see if see if there are fresh opportunities for faith hidden within those disruptions. As a result, God keeps finding fresh ways to shake up our complacencies and, as far as depression goes, challenge us to resist the seductive temptation to play the victim.

One of depression's more insidious deceptions is to trick us into colluding with our captor, to give up and give in to depression's tight grip. Acting with graced resolve, however, calls us out of victimhood and leads us to seize the strength we need to push the stone away from depression's dark tomb, making way for resurrection's hoped-for dawn.

But sometimes we really are depression's victims. Disarmed of will and desire, we're outmaneuvered by darkness and deprived of the energy to push anything aside. When we hit this wall, we reluctantly need to shelve our pride and unending determination to fix ourselves, and remember that spiritual growth sometimes means humbly letting God do the heavy lifting. Just being sad in God's presence often proves a most reliable path to healing and resurrection. That's when God can show us that our lives are larger than our depression, and that God's life is big enough to embrace them both.

Learning to distinguish between suffering and pain also helps. Suffering can be redemptive; it's part of the soul's work of embracing love. When we suffer well, a gentle, inexplicable hope sustains and leads us—usually more slowly than we would like—into growth and redemption.

Pain, on the other hand, just hurts; it goes nowhere and simply breeds static resentment and resignation, the tools of dark hopelessness. Jesus seems to have known this difference well, because the Gospels are full of stories showing him driving out painful demons and offering hope in a love that has forged a tentative kinship with suffering and joy. When depression strikes, we live on a continuum between embracing the suffering that can lead to life and holding at bay the pain that just keeps us in bondage.

Don't ever let anybody tell you that depression and the dark night experiences described by the mystics are the same thing. Depression is nothing but pain and we need to get out of it; the dark night is a grace that we enter into with God.

Most of us probably wish that our fidelity to the process of spiritual growth would absolve us of illness and suffering, worry and doubt, depression and loneliness. Our faith shows us that suffering is a permanent part of our lives, but discernment leads us to distinguish between suffering and pain. Excluding suffering from our experience leads us to a theoretical sense of self. Our faith, however, is never just theory.

| SILENT SOUNDS |

When we want to learn how to pray, we seek people who are friends of God to teach us or spend time in places of prayer like monasteries. Monasteries draw me like a magnet, and I've driven out of my way and over tricky roads to visit some of them. Each monastery has its own brand of silence, born of its spiritual heritage and formed by the people who live there. Silence helps creates the holy space we need to listen to God.

When I moved to Minnesota, I began visiting St. John's Abbey in Collegeville. It's the place that championed liturgical renewal on the backs of Minnesota farm boys turned monks and scholars.

The first time I attended evening prayer there I expected to hear lots of chant echoing off the hard, dark gray concrete walls of the church. What I experienced, however, was very different, and that difference has made a long-standing impact on me. The way these monks celebrate the Liturgy of the Hours is stark, almost barren. There's some singing, but mostly the psalms are spoken slowly and deliberately, with long pauses between each of them.

I found the slow pace unnerving at first; it irritated my addictive need to be busy and productive. One of the monks told me that for all the activity of the community, praying slowly and deliberately had a way of slowing things down for them and their guests.

I've always felt at home in the psalms, so I decided to imitate alone how the monks at St. John's pray the psalms together. I started reading them slowly out loud, and felt self-conscious and almost embarrassed praying them that way all by myself. I had to resist my tendency to read quickly, but most of all, I had to outgrow a tendency to pray the way I lived rather than allowing prayer shape the way I lived. An unexpected payoff in praying this way was that it slowed me down in general, gradually helping me welcome the silences and pauses I needed to live more reflectively.

I still read the psalms like this every day, and there are days when it works well and other days when I almost have to strap myself in my chair when my personal atoms want to move at warp speed. Making a commitment to do this independently of how I feel at a particular time every day, however, has become an anchor in my life. It's something like going to the gym for me: If I don't do it in the morning, it's not going to happen.

Using the psalms in prayer is a practice I'd encourage you to explore. Knowing that Jesus prayed the psalms means we're in good company when we start to use them. The psalms are a prayer book and a school of prayer for Jews and Christians, enjoying a privileged place in the public prayer of both traditions. They can also give voice to the joys and sorrows you and I experience in the hard work of spiritual growth. Start to pray them and prepare to be amazed.

Let me suggest how you might get started with the psalms. There's a Responsorial Psalm every day between the first and second readings in the liturgy. Start with this psalm and read it slowly out loud (don't just read it to yourself), noting words or expressions that speak to you in a comforting or challenging way (underline them as a way of committing yourself to them). Read the psalm again and pause at these places again and others that may strike you the second time through.

Spend time in silence at these places and listen for the word that God may want to speak to you. Keep track of the word that God seems to be speaking to you, and over time you may start to see a pattern. Use the Responsorial Psalm this way for at least a month or two.

When you feel comfortable with the psalms, read all 150 of them prayerfully, in order, without any particular need to read the longer psalms in one day. I often suggest that people mark those psalms that especially command their attention, noting which ones comfort you and which ones challenge you. Then you have your own personal psalm prayer book that you can come back to for a long time before you begin the process all over again.

The psalms span the entire human emotional and spiritual range—from anger and contempt, fear and hope, to petition and adoration. They may even give us permission to say things to God we may have always thought were off-limits in prayer. We're the ones, however, who have decided what parts of our experience can and can't be brought to God. Fortunately, God doesn't know that rule.

Depression has come out of the closet, but loneliness is still hiding in there, out of sight and out of mind. If you practice the fine art of just happening to overhear conversations, you'll eventually hear people talk about the antidepressants they take. It's almost a badge of honor. A friend told me how stunned he was when he found out that everybody in his support group takes the same medication. I have to admit that I occasionally take extravagant pleasure in telling people that I ingest enough medication to brighten the mood of my entire neighborhood.

We've learned how to talk about depression, but can you remember the last time somebody admitted to you that they really felt trapped in loneliness? Statistics say it doesn't happen with any real frequency. The big year for books about loneliness was 2010. Emily White's book *Lonely* appeared then, followed by *Lonely in America*, and *Loneliness as a Way of Life*.

A common theme in all these books is that loneliness, unlike depression, still carries a stigma: Being lonely is a person's fault, a weakness, or a personality deficit. Get over it. We stand a better chance of treating ourselves compassionately if we're depressed rather than lonely. Loneliness prompts its own nasty brand of personal contempt.

I take a skeptical view of dressing up loneliness in the language of solitude or aloneness, just as I do when I hear depression described as the dark night of the soul. Loneliness, solitude, and aloneness are each quite different, and thinking of them as the same can confuse and hurt us. We can call loneliness anything we want, but, in the end, we're still lonely.

Lonely people make lousy hermits. For successful solitaries, aloneness is a way of connecting rather than disconnecting from others or the world. Aloneness has as little to do with loneliness as introversion has to do with shyness. Being alone without being overtaken by loneliness is what people who aren't lonely know how to do. But being alone threatens the lonely. Being dangerously low on connections, lonely folks feel left out, overlooked, always on the outside looking in, constantly playing the victim or trying to figure out what's wrong with them.

I've lived inside depression and loneliness myself, and, although I'm not a clinical expert on either, I bristle at glib proclamations like, "Once I embraced my loneliness, everything got better." I tried to embrace my depression and loneliness for a long time and failed. Embracing loneliness or depression is a good first step, but it can never be the only step.

What about our relationship with God when we're lonely? Can we be chronically lonely yet experience authentic intimacy with God? Only a fool would attempt a definitive answer to this question, but I would venture a tentative, "I doubt it." All of our relationships tend to parallel each other, and, when they don't, I get nervous — something just isn't right.

What I'm suggesting is that lonely people, especially those in spiritual direction or in other ways involved in spiritual growth, might want to examine the quality of all their relationships calmly, resolutely, and compassionately. This kind of reflection is done best in conversation with another, rather than in the confining silence of our own heads.

The psalms teem with images of what it feels like to be lonely, to be cut off from God and others. There's a primal fear in them of being forgotten by God, left alone to face the predators that prowl around us alone and unprotected, being invisible, forgotten, and ultimately making no difference to anyone, including ourselves.

The psalmist often talks about feeling like the dead, with no lifelines in hand or even in sight. To get a sense of this, read Psalm 88. But other psalms speak of being rescued by God, returned from exile, finally finding a homeland.

But what's the game plan for finally getting past the place where loneliness holds us hostage? Getting professional help when we need it is a given, but can spiritual sensitivity and prayer help us in this process?

Experience has shown me that making progress in managing loneliness is similar to learning how to move through depression. When we speak of our loneliness or depression to another, or, in the case of prayer, to The Other, we can be slowly shown that we aren't defined by either, that we are larger than our feelings. It's in this larger space that healing happens; we just need to keep it open for business.

As the healing gaze of God gives us the hope and courage to break our attachment to these feelings, God then has a chance to invite us into the spacious freedom that is God's great gift. Freedom, imagination, and trust are gifts the Holy Spirit brings us. Living in them faithfully is the best chance to have to discover and embrace new ways of being with God, self, and others. This is when it finally dawns on us that embracing loneliness or depression is only the first of many steps into being more fully alive.

I remember quite well the quiet morning when I finally came to the simple realization that I didn't feel overwhelmed by depression; it no longer seemed so heavy. The same thing happened with loneliness. One day I made a mental list of concrete steps I had taken to combat loneliness, and saw that I indeed had been moving in that direction. It just took much longer for my brain to catch up with the activity of my heart.

The psalms work like that too. There's usually a pause between the lament and the prayer of thanksgiving. That's when we can look back and see how God has never left us alone. It also inspires the hope we need to rely on God's fidelity in the future. Psalm 116 is a good sacred song to sing from time to time.

Bill Lynch—that's William F. Lynch, S.J., who wrote *Christ and Apollo, Images of Faith,* and *Images of Hope,* among other books— was astonishingly brilliant and just as amazingly difficult to get along with. We lived in the same community early on in my Jesuit career and, for some reason or other, we got along. Brilliance certainly didn't cement the bond, so it must have been a shared grouchiness. Or it may have been the bottle of Martell I had in my room. Whatever the reason, Bill liked to stop by my room at night, enjoy a snifter of brandy, and talk about his life and what he was writing.

One night he told me what occasioned his book *Images of Hope.* He had suffered a serious mental collapse, and then spent time as a patient at St. Elizabeth Hospital, a psychiatric facility in Washington, DC. He started to get better, he told me, when he was finally able to sense that his life could be different. "My imagination started to come back to life," he said, "and I no longer felt checkmated by hopelessness—possibilities became real for me again." That's why the full title of his book reads *Images of Hope: Imagination as Healer of the Hopeless.*

Fast-forward about twenty years to when I worked in executive outplacement. One of my early clients was a red-haired, fifty-something engineer who had worked for a company for thirty years. He was remarkably angry that he had lost his job—so angry, in fact, that our receptionist asked me to let her know when has was coming in so she could take her break at the same time.

He had done precision tooling for an engineering company, and he kept talking about how his boss ripped his heart out when he was downsized. His anger finally reached the boiling point when he realized he had worked at his job before he was married or had kids. At this point he was just looking for reasons to be angry: It had become his transition object.

One morning, he told me about a crazy idea he had during the past week. I jumped on the comment and asked him what happened. "It was just a crazy idea I had in the garage on Friday, not really anything worth talking about," he said. Being prompted, perhaps, as much by impatience as well as by curiosity, I said, "Well, tell me about it." "When I was in the garage it dawned on me that I have all the equipment I would need to do on my own the kind of tooling work I did for the company. Isn't that crazy?"

As tentative and crazy as it seemed to him, this was the first time in months he had a glimmer of a way out of the rat maze he had been living in way too long. In the background, I could hear Bill Lynch talking about the imagination coming back to life and bringing a glimmer of hope with it.

"What makes you think it's such a crazy idea?" I asked him. "I don't know," he said, "it's just something I never thought about before." In true consulting style, I urged him to think about what he had said. "Can we talk about this again next week?" I asked. "I guess so," he said. We concluded our session by agreeing to meet again the following Monday.

When we got together the next week, he seemed a bit more buoyant, even a bit less angry. "So what do you think about your idea from last week?" I asked. "You know," he said, "it probably wasn't as crazy as it thought. I've got the equipment and thirty years' worth of people who know the quality of my work. I can't start my own business tomorrow, but I think I ought to check it out—maybe I could make it happen in a year or so."

He ultimately decided on a plan to go out on his own even as he looked for another traditional job, but just welcoming the possibility transformed his imagination, sparking creativity and even hope. He lacked a business plan, but at least he had an idea.

Ignatius Loyola had a similar experience as he recuperated from his leg injury. God had graced him with an idea of how his life might be different, but, at that point, Ignatius, too, didn't have a business plan—a picture of how that idea might take flesh.

We start to move out of loss—our Holy Saturday time—when we accept out of God's gracious hand a word of possibility and life. Then we wait more actively for the word to become flesh in our own lives.

Have you ever noticed how yesterday's great idea sometimes become today's even bigger regret? The hard-core regulars at my gym joke about the "resolutions," people who excitedly buy memberships in December, show up for a week or two in January, and are never seen again. In the interest of full disclosure, I have to admit that a few of them stick it out and become regulars, but most of the resolutions just keep membership costs low for the rest of us.

Some people suffering from depression take antidepressants to brighten their mood and, in many cases, they get their lives back. Others stop taking meds when they feel better because they don't think they need them any longer. But stopping medications abruptly can cause a person to crash, leaving them feeling even more deeply depressed. It's like standing on a ladder and having it knocked out from under you—the crash is sudden, frightening, and dangerous.

There are some people, however, who stop taking antidepressants because they feel better with the medication. As counterintuitive as that may seem, they've never felt good before and when they start to, it scares them. They know how to live with depression but don't have a clue how to live without it. Although depression is dark and lonely, its addictive payoffs are often safety and predictability. Some of us are skilled in cannibalizing change however it shows up.

Every once in a while, I wonder whether getting a miraculous cure from Jesus may have triggered similar reactions. Some of the leprous, blind, and paralyzed who were cured by Jesus certainly got busy right away taking advantage of their new lease on life. There had to be others, however, who were just as excited about the idea of being cured but, once they were, wound up scared to death by the chaos the change might unleash in their lives. After all, the blind knew how to be blind, lepers knew how to live alone, and the paralyzed knew how to live without mobility. Life may have been hard, but it was bearable because it was familiar.

But the day after the miracle, the blind couldn't make a living begging anymore, lepers had to learn how to live with others, and paralytics had to walk for themselves. Dependency is often easier than independence, and blaming our situation on someone or something else can feel more comfortable than assuming responsibility.

Soon after the Israelites escaped slavery, they screamed at Moses for leading them out into the desert to die. They were slaves in Egypt, but they were slaves with full bellies. Similarly, we may also fall in love with the idea of change one day, without considering the tough changes that await us the next.

The Gospels are full of sober warnings for potential disciples of Jesus. Don't be fooled, Jesus tells them, into thinking the disciple's road is placid and serene, or that God will make everything pleasant, perfect, or easy. All we're consistently offered is a chance to take up our cross every day and follow Jesus.

Accepting the cross doesn't mean we just get used to feeling pain. It does mean that we need to shoulder the responsibility for the hard work of being a disciple with our eyes wide open. Only suffering love leads to resurrected life.

Ignatius Loyola reminds us in the *Spiritual Exercises* that "Love ought to be placed rather in works than in words," something he may have learned listening to Jesus tell his disciples, "Not everyone who says to me, 'Lord, Lord' will enter the kingdom of heaven, but only the one who does the will of my Father in heaven" (Matthew 7:21). Doing God's will, we learn, means we actually do something about making it real. That kind of person, Jesus argues, is like the savvy person who builds a house on rock. Dorothy Day once reminded us that love in reality is a harsh and dreadful thing. It can be really scary.

Before we enthusiastically fall in love with the idea of spiritual growth, we'd better make sure we're prepared to accept responsibility for what it might demand of us. Making a commitment to pray every morning sounds like a great idea until we have to drag ourselves out of bed early the next morning.

On the other hand, we also need to remember that some mornings we're just better off if we stay in bed—sometimes we need sleep more than prayer. And then there's that person we don't like who asks for our help at an inconvenient time. There are other times, however, when we need to ask somebody to help us, but pride and a false sense of self-reliance hold us back.

Fidelity in discipleship calls us out of our self-centered fear and into the self-forgetting world we see in Jesus. We're called to live—not just think about—discipleship. That way, fidelity, trust, and action may turn the day after the miracle into a celebration of life for us.

When I was growing up, all the kids in my neighborhood—all the boys, I should say—learned the ins and outs of heroism from comic books. We read *Superman* comics religiously and watched on television as he defeated evildoers while repeatedly rescuing Lois Lane and Jimmy Olson. We wanted to be like Superman more than anything.

We became superheroes when we played, each of us determined to outdo the other in pretend valor. Our imaginations helped us step into the superhero's world, and it was there that we developed a taste for saving and rescuing. But play is serious work: In it we try on different roles, experiment with new behaviors, and store up what we learn in our imaginations.

Watch a *Superman* or *Star Wars* film, or an episode of *Xena: Warrior Princess* and see what emotions stir in you. We never get tired of stories about larger-than-life figures using superhuman power to protect the weak, resist tyranny, and restore order. These kinds of stories connect us with parts of ourselves.

Ignatius Loyola loved reading stories about knights who distinguished themselves as heroes in the service of their lords and ladies. A soldier himself before his leg was shattered, the only available reading during his recuperation was the lives of the saints. To tame his boredom, he read them just like stories about knights. Imagination took him inside the lives of the saints, and he gradually came to see them as God's great heroes—men and women he admired and wanted to imitate. The saints did extraordinary deeds of love and service because they wanted to be like Jesus. Suddenly, Ignatius wanted to be like the saints more than anything.

Ignatius read Gospel stories the same way, and it developed into a prayer practice called Ignatian Gospel contemplation. In this kind of prayer, Ignatius imagined himself in the Gospel scene and became an active participant in it, not just a detached observer. As grace touched his heart, he was transformed from a self-obsessed soldier into a selfless disciple of Jesus. Ignatius wanted to be like Jesus, and he incorporated this kind of prayer into the *Spiritual Exercises* because of that desire.

Why do stories have the power to change and convert? Part of the reason is that they touch our feelings and motivation, not just our thinking and reasoning. Once our imaginations get involved, the Gospel story can become part of the story of our lives. That's how we identify with Jesus, and, more importantly, that's how Jesus identifies with us. What happens is a meeting of hearts, not just a meeting of minds.

Early in the *Spiritual Exercises* we are invited to imagine ourselves in a Gospel scene that is as lovely as it is intimate and potentially life changing. Imagine being with Mary and Joseph just after Jesus has been born and placed in the manger. What are Mary and Joseph saying? What do you see in their eyes and on their faces? Where are you in the scene? What do you want to say? To whom? What's it like for you to see Jesus as a helpless infant? Imagine Mary or Joseph handing Jesus to you for comfort when he cries.

Let the scene get under your skin. Where is this suggested in your own experience? For example, what is God bringing to birth in you? How has new life been handed to you to nurture and grow? What does this new life ask of you? What does it offer you? What feelings does it awaken? Spend time speaking with the Lord "as one friend to another," in the words of Ignatius. Remember, prayer is a conversation, not a monologue. Give God a chance to speak life into the story of your life. What might God be calling you to be or do?

Pray this way with a favorite Gospel story. Why is it a favorite? Why does it grab your attention time after time? How does it console and challenge you? Where do you see yourself in it? Who else is there? What do they say to you? What do you say? Where are you in relation to Jesus? What does Jesus say to you and what do you say in return? Spend some time to see if you have a similar story burning in your heart.

Try reading Mark's Gospel, for instance, and note which stories console you, which challenge you, and which confuse you. Live inside these stories and allow the Lord to open a place of transformation and conversion. Don't be tempted by abstraction: Stay in the concrete experience of your life in these stories, allowing them to suggest rather than tell. Let them lead you into your own story of grace, conversion, and healing.

This is where God will meet you. And God wants this more than anything.

The Feast of Christ the King used to scare all my classmates and me when we were in the early grades in Catholic elementary school. We didn't know how it happened, but that's when the larger-than-life Sacred Heart statue in the church turned into Christ the King for one day. To mark the occasion, the statue was suitably outfitted in a red velvet robe with imitation ermine piping, a plastic crown, and a scepter duct-taped into its bloody, nail-pierced right hand.

Since Christmas wasn't too far off, here was a guy, we figured, who really could tell if we had been naughty or nice, and we knew we risked getting the punishment we deserved for being bad. At that point in our lives, however, the threat of spending eternity in hell was less motivating than the fear of not getting the Christmas gifts we wanted. Thus was born an image that rattled around inside my head for years to come: Christ as no-nonsense ruler and divine avenger.

The statue suffered an undignified death by wrecking ball when the old church was torn down, and my image of God has grown more compassionate and loving as I grow older. But the statue—both as Sacred Heart and Christ the King—is still a part of my religious memory.

During the past few years, however, the image of Christ as avenger of evil has been resurrected, especially among some more traditional Catholics. They think of themselves as orthodox rather than

73

traditionalist, but their theology and the judgments they make have all the brittle impersonality of the Church before the Second Vatican Council.

As the ecclesial cultural wars heat up between traditionalist and progressive ways of thinking and living, people of my ilk are labeled dissenters and advised by the supposedly more orthodox not to receive Communion until we repent and reject our evil ways. Remember, they say, God is in control and will, in God's own calculated time, run all the enemies of truth and good out of town. Consider yourself warned.

As I so gallantly sit atop my own high horse, I have to admit that I revel in thinking the same way. Disagree with my religious views, and my side will instantly label your side small-minded and ignorant, and ridicule your theological and political perspectives as benighted or just plain ill-informed.

The sad truth is that when any of us trade faith for ideology, the gutter becomes our home and bickering and name-calling our blood sport. That's when everything and everybody is caricatured as either black or white, winners or losers, enlightened or ignorant, saint or sinner with a surgical precision that's as illusory as it is inhuman.

As the fighting rages today, however, Christianity itself seldom winds up in the winner's circle. Instead, don't we see Christians, whether traditionalist or progressive, increasingly marginalized and enduring persecution, ridicule, and suffering? Famed American Protestant theologian Reinhold Niebuhr once wrote that Christians often want a victorious love, yet what we really get, he wisely cautioned, is a God who comes in suffering love, disarmingly seen in Jesus, the person of sorrow and eternal companion of powerlessness and humiliation.

Suffering can redeem and transform, but it seldom wins. Instead, we share the intimate knowledge of Paul the apostle that we are a people afflicted but never crushed, confused but never despairing, knocked down but always getting to our feet, taken for dead, but here we are alive. Most of our resurrections are hushed and even tentative, always born of a divine suffering love that offers only fragile healing and hope.

This is when I remember the statue I knew as a kid. Perhaps we dress Jesus in the trappings of fake royalty so we don't have to face what's hidden under all the pretend: nothing but a vulnerable, sacred heart pieced for us. After all, it's God's wounded love for us that gives us the strength to strip away our personal disguises and winner-take-all ideology, only to find our own wounded heart, the vulnerable part of our truth we don't like to face, much less embrace. Jesus, it turns out, was recognized after the resurrection most often only in his wounds.

Despite all our ideological grandstanding, we are invited to recognize our suffering Church in its identification with the wounded Christ. We shouldn't be deluded into thinking that this will resolve the differences among the factions we see in today's Church. They're entrenched and volatile, and will not go away instantly or magically.

In fact, they may not go away at all, and our call might be to live with people with whom we have differences of the heart. But just learning to live together without trying to change the minds of those who disagree with us is one of the hard tasks of Christian discipleship. In the process, we'll be better off imitating the Sacred Heart side of the statue.

Only sinners have the patience to listen to the stories Jesus tells. The self-righteous hear them but don't listen. Hearing happens when the ears and the brain team up, but listening happens with the ears of the heart. Listening is personal, involving, and intimate; hearing is impersonal, abstract, and detached.

Since sinners like us can listen to the stories Jesus tells, you and I have the chance to listen with the ears of our hearts to the fifteenth chapter of Luke's Gospel. In it Luke shows how God is always waiting on tiptoe looking for lost sheep, lost coins, and even lost sons. Listen attentively and we'll find our place in each of them. All three stories have one plotline: seeking, returning, and celebrating.

The first two verses of the chapter (Luke 15:1–2) show the difference between hearing and listening. We're told, "the tax collectors and sinners were coming near to listen to him." One translation says they were "leaning in" close to him. At the same time, "the Pharisees and the scribes were grumbling and saying, 'This fellow welcomes sinners and eats with them.'" The company Jesus kept offended them.

Disciples are imperfect people—tax collectors and sinners—who lean in to hear good news from Jesus. Leaning in to listen to him is also a decent description of prayer. Our Christian life is the back and forth between leaning in toward Jesus and leaning away from the voices of self-righteousness we see in the Pharisees and scribes.

Spend enough time in prayer with Jesus, and we can learn how to embrace the grace of listening before judging. Our interior Pharisee evaluates without listening to a word. Why bother? The truth is already clear; it just needs to be applied to life. Prayer, however, is how faith listens, leaning in toward Jesus, always open to the eternal ambiguity of surprise and creativity, healing and hope.

One of the movements in prayer is listening to Jesus. That's what meditation does: It reflects on God's Word in the presence of God and applies what we learn to our lives. The Christian tradition describes this as "discursive" prayer because we use reasoning power in prayer.

There's something disturbing in the spiritual air today that tries to convince us that reflective prayer is low-level: Real prayer happens without thinking or even words. Unfortunately, God doesn't seem to have gotten the memo to this effect. If reflective prayer helps you grow in faith, hope, and love, keep doing it. Praying without thoughts or words is a gift, not something we do for ourselves in prayer.

There may come a time in our prayer life when all our efforts at reflective prayer seem in vain. One reason this might happen—but certainly not the only reason—is that God may be leading us to pray with Jesus. As we listen more to Jesus in prayer and Scripture, we may slowly grow in the quality of our discipleship, the grace of being with Jesus in his ministry of reconciliation.

That's when we learn to listen with Jesus to the words of life offered by God. In other words, our prayer moves us back and forth between listening *to* Jesus and listening *with* Jesus. When we pray with Jesus, his prayer and our own begin to become one. Not only does the disciple take on the mind of Christ, the disciple slowly takes on the will and zeal of Jesus for ministry. It's discerning prayer: How and where are we called and supported in laboring with Christ?

There is still another movement in prayer: leaning in close to pray in Jesus. There's more to any relationship than learning about somebody we love, more even than being with that person in the ups and downs of living with each other. Praying in Jesus is the simple presence of the silent Holy Mystery of God dwelling in and beyond our humanity. This calls for a union of hearts as well as thinking and acting. We learn to be "hidden with Christ in God" (Colossians 3:3).

Don't we also experience this when we've been around somebody long enough that we've heard most of their thoughts? Or we've worked with somebody long enough to get a sense of how they respond to questions, needs, and crises?

Then there's the connection that comes just from presence: listening to music together, going out to dinner together, or even just watching TV with one another. This is the kind of familiar intimacy that strengthens and touches us, deepens our love, and sometimes makes patience easy. When our frenetic minds finally come to rest and the day's work is over, aren't we just left with each other in silence, without need for words?

Don't you agree that we're always listening to, with, and in Jesus? We're always leaning in to listen to Jesus in word, service, and simple, loving presence.

American novelist David Foster Wallace committed suicide in 2008, but I became familiar with him after his death. I happened onto his biography quite by chance, bought it, and devoured it in two days. Then I tackled all 1,079 pages of his gargantuan novel, *Infinite Jest*, making a vow to read ten pages of it every day for four months until I finished.

That's when I became part of an elite group of those who have read the book but still have no real idea what it was really about. I can give you a plot summary, but what kept me going back for more every day was the raw, addictive quality of Wallace's prose. It's sweltering, taut, visceral.

Wallace relied on support groups to keep his substance abuse problems in check. In interviews I watched on YouTube, he spoke about the deadening effect of drugs and nonstop entertainment on lives. He admitted he couldn't own a TV; if he did, he'd watch it all the time. And if he drank, he'd drink all the time too. But it was depression that finally did him in.

At the end of the interview, he admitted with a smirk that most of the trouble he got into in his life stemmed from his confusion about what he wanted and what he needed. Getting rid of all pain as fast as possible became his obsession, and he rarely put up with it long enough for it to be transfigured. It was the simple outcome of capitalist marketing, he figured—making money on the "technologies of escape"—and it amounted to a simple contractual exchange. In exchange for my soul, I'll pay money to erase my pain immediately. As we practice being disciples of Jesus, we also run into the informal contracts we've made with the death-dealing dimensions of our culture. Recognizing our own technologies of escape is part and parcel of discipleship in the twenty-first century. Taking our lead from Wallace, we also need to take seriously the incessant barrage of quick fixes peddled by our culture.

Too much of what passes for spirituality is an almost addictive focus on our interior lives. No spirituality today can afford to be so lopsided. One movement of spirituality is to turn inward, but it's just as important to come back outside. It's grace that can keep us balanced and prevent us from getting stuck in either place. But let's spend time reflecting on the outside dimension of our lives, where we also stand a good chance of getting in trouble, just like David Foster Wallace.

The disciples of Jesus assess all their relationships with people, points of view, and things against the Gospel standard of graced freedom. We're always on the lookout for which relationships free us and which enslave us. It's from this perspective that we might want to pray about our relationship with advertising and consumerism. Do we ever pray about this? Do we know when we confuse what we want with what we need? Undisciplined, unredeemed desires can get us in trouble before we even know what's going on.

How often do you and I pray about our society's involvement with violence and war? What about our systemic involvement in keeping the poor and powerless in their place, not to mention racism, homophobia, and ageism? And then there's gun violence, and discrimination in education and jobs. It's all part of another list that could go on forever. I bring this all up not just to make us feel guilty, but to recognize the unfortunate landscape in which our faith has to be practiced.

Sometimes I wonder why my silence is so noisy, and then I think of how often I turn to noise for companionship or to drown out my panic when nothing's going on. No wonder my prayer bounces from one thought and image to another. Food is also a good way to keep sadness at bay—so is activity, work, sex, or the Internet. What are your favorite technologies of escape? Take the time you need to identify them. Be specific, and don't get pulled into the greatest lie of self-reflection—generalization.

Not long ago, I attended a gathering of spiritual directors, and we were asked to discuss the challenges facing spirituality today. After all the groups reported their discussions, not one group had mentioned the necessary link between faith and justice. We can't afford to be held hostage by a dangerous spirituality that has the leisure and self-absorption to think spirituality is just about our insides.

Famed business writer Jim Collins introduced the "Stockdale Paradox" in his blockbuster book *Good to Great*. There he reintroduced us to Rear Admiral James Stockdale, the decorated Vietnam War hero who was Ross Perot's pick for vice president in his unsuccessful run for president in 1992.

Stockdale, a navy aviator, was shot down over Vietnam in 1965 and spent the next seven years as a prisoner of war in what was called the "Hanoi Hilton." He was the highest-ranking naval officer in the prison and is credited with keeping many of his fellow prisoners alive and sane.

Collins says he got depressed reading about Stockdale's ordeal, even though he knew that Stockdale finally got out of prison. What he couldn't figure out, however, was how Stockdale survived not knowing the endgame, so he interviewed him when he was writing *Good to Great*. Collins wanted to know about the people who never got out of prison alive, and Stockdale's now-famous response that the optimists always died is what gave birth to what Collins eventually termed the Stockdale Paradox.

The optimists, he explained, were always unrealistic, Stockdale claimed. They magically figured they'd get out by Christmas, and when that didn't happen, they set their hearts on Easter. They died from broken hearts when nothing worked out the way they expected it would.

Stockdale never said anything about what happened to the pessimists, but I'll bet they also died. The optimists died of disappointment, but I'll bet the pessimists died of hopelessness. In any case, neither way of thinking and living proved realistic, and ultimately both proved fatal.

According to the Stockdale Paradox, the prisoners who survived were those who could face the hard facts of their imprisonment while simultaneously being convinced that despite it all, they would prevail in the end. They traded in naïve optimism for hard-nosed hope, and dark pessimism for balanced realism. It's a clear story about how what I've called binocular vision can save and heal.

Using the Stockdale Paradox as a guide, we might get a fresh perspective on what's traditionally called the parable of the Prodigal Son in the Gospel of Luke (15:11–32). The parable has also been called the parable of the Two Sons or even the parable of the Waiting Father.

However we get to the story's heart, its meaning is intimately tied to the matrix of human relationships revealed: father to each son and to both sons, the ties of each son and both sons to their father, and the relationship between the two sons. Despite its original all-male cast, I find it helpful to alternate the genders of the characters. There's a pervasive feminine presence in the story that we ignore at our own peril.

Think of the impetuous son—the prodigal—as the pessimist, and the dutiful older son as the optimist. The younger son sees himself as irredeemable, no longer even worthy to be called a son. He's filled with despair. But the older son sees himself as responsible, certainly taken for granted. He hasn't screwed up like his kid brother. While the younger son's poison may be self-derision and despair, the older son's drug of choice is pride and self-righteousness. I hate to admit it, but lots of times I think the older brother got a raw deal.

That's when it's clear how little I know of God. I expect God to play by my rules, and I get angry when God doesn't act that way. The only thing the prodigal's father knows how to do is love without our rules. Although I understand the story, it intimidates me at a much deeper level. Whether we see ourselves as unlovable or as entitled to love, God has been impatiently waiting for us, ready to rush toward us and save us from ourselves.

As many commentators on this Scripture story have pointed out, we don't know how the story turns out. Were the sons able to accept the father's love? Were the two sons eventually able to reconcile? If I slowly let this story interpret my life, however, I start to see both sons living inside me and constantly wrestling each other to gain exclusive access to my heart.

The question we all face is whether we'll allow divine arms to hold us and comfort us. Can we find it in ourselves to let go of cheap optimism and pessimism to find hard-won hope instead? Just as we don't know how the prodigal son story ended, we don't know for sure if we'll choose love over despair and self-righteousness, life over death. We can only pray to be faithful to grace.

Maybe it's good that we don't know how things finally turn out. This is the kind of a story that is never completed in thinking—only in living.

Without a doubt, Berlin is my favorite European city. I used to go there for business and pleasure — mostly pleasure, I have to admit. The city was a staging area for much of worst and some of the best of the twentieth century. Stay there long enough and you'll start to absorb the sense of cataclysm that pervaded Europe after World War II, something usually lost on Americans.

The city was Nazism's hub, and many of the atrocities of the Third Reich were planned there. Hitler committed suicide there and, by war's end, much of the city had been obliterated by Allied bombs. After Nazism came communism, and its chokehold on half the city culminated in the erection of the Berlin Wall in the early 1960s.

And after the Wall was ripped down piece by piece, Berlin became a symbol of the slow resurgence of hope, freedom, and democracy, not only for the city, but for much of Eastern Europe. I was a kid when the Wall went up and shared in the global sigh of relief when it was finally turned into dust.

I spent Good Friday in Berlin one year and was trying to figure out how to observe it religiously. Most of that morning was spent wandering up and down the Kufürstendamm, West Berlin's fashionable main street, but I wound up in the Kaiser Wilhelm Memorial Church in the early afternoon. I was in the right place at the right time.

Much of the church was destroyed during the war, but when the time came for rebuilding, the new church was built into and around what was left of the old church. The church's bombed and broken spire is an eerie reminder of the war's destructiveness, a memory the Germans felt obligated to keep alive.

After sitting in the church for at least an hour, I came to see that I was spending Good Friday in the very heart of the passion, death, and resurrection of Jesus, the slow yet startling victory of life and hope over death and hatred. Right there, in that church, it was impossible to take the mystery of our redemption for granted or intellectualize it. Faith also has to surrender any vestiges of romanticism there. Confronting the reality of evil in our world without collapsing in cynicism and despair is a gritty test for the realism of our faith.

Charles Gibson interviewed Archbishop Desmond Tutu in the early 2000s, and asked him if he didn't think the twentieth century had witnessed every conceivable evil known to humankind. Tutu thought for a minute and then said, "That's true, Charlie, but it's not the whole picture. The twentieth century was also the occasion of great grace. We can't forget that." What a staggering message of hope from somebody who has certainly seen the best and worst of how people can treat teach other.

A couple of years ago, I was privileged to spend time with a South African Episcopal priest, Michael Lapsley. He had publicly supported an end to apartheid in South Africa, and, as a result, both his hands were blown off when he opened a letter bomb. He is another person who has been saved by hope, and, as a result, he gives workshops around the world on the healing of memories.

My dad also showed me something of this hope. He was physician who would often leave dinner early to take care of migrant workers who did seasonal harvesting and were housed in camps run by the companies that owned the large farms. Even as a kid, I knew he never got paid, but it wasn't until after he died that I learned he had received death threats for going into the camps. But he never stopped going.

All of this came rushing into my heart that Good Friday afternoon in Berlin. Even today when we witness the unspeakable evil and human carnage throughout the world—including here, in the United States—we might well be tempted to give up on grace. Closer to home, I'm also sometimes tempted to give up on grace when I repeatedly see the evil I'm capable of perpetrating.

Using Archbishop Tutu's observation of always seeing good and evil together, however, we might do well to chronicle for ourselves our heroes in grace. Spend time to remember and appreciate the people in your life who, despite it all, kept you hopeful as you encountered situations of evil, suffering, and sadness. See, too, the love and grace that touches all our lives in these situations.

That's when I remember Good Friday in Berlin, Desmond Tutu, Michael Lapsley, and my dad. They tried to teach me not to give up on hope for the world or even for myself. After all, the only God we know is all too familiar with the cost of suffering love.

PART THREE

NOW

WHAT?

Dilemmas

of

Discernment

When British-born painter David Hockney moved to California in the 1960s, he painted a series of acrylics that came to be known as his "pool paintings." One of them still grabs my imagination. In it is a swimming pool sparkling with three shades of blue water, seen from a yellow diving board. I imagine a person standing there, just out of sight, perpetually caught in that nanosecond between deciding and acting.

Hockney's painting reminds me of lazy, sunny days as a kid, when my friends and I spent aimless hours at the local swimming pool. We learned to dive off the lower board—the springboard—the same summer we started jumping from the high dive. But jumping wasn't enough, and I was determined to dive from the high dive that summer, just as soon as I mustered the courage I needed to take the leap and not just think about it.

Our swimming coach, Mr. Pope, must have sensed this, because one afternoon he followed me up the high dive, sat behind me on the board, and held my ankles so I wouldn't fall. I couldn't see him, but knowing he was there gave me the reassurance I needed to take a risk and dive. Actually, he gave me the push I needed to dive off the board and into the water. Staring at the water wasn't enough; I had to dive in deep and come back out of the water amazingly still alive, beaming with boyish pride.

Living in God's presence and keeping our eyes open for opportunities to love and be loved, serve and be served, are never quite enough, are they? Don't we finally need to dive in and get wet, taking a chance that God will keep us safe and bring us out of the baptismal waters of service and love more fully alive? God's spirit is the Mr. Pope of our souls, always encouraging but also constantly nudging us to turn the warm idea of love into the hard work of service and self-forgetting love.

When I worked as a career management consultant, I hung Hockney's painting in my office. Job seekers also reach a point when strategizing has to give way to sustained, focused activity. That's when the phone calls start, company research is done, and networking meetings happen with only one goal: getting interviews.

Hockney's pool painting is the last work of art I offer for your reflection and prayer. First came Emerson Burkhart's self-portrait, a personal image of what God's loving care might look like. Robert Mapplethorpe's photograph of Tim Scott then showed us that being seen in love by God compels us to imitate God in scanning the horizon to find fresh opportunities for faith, hope, and love. Just like prayer, putting ourselves at the service of others is a time-tested way for us to find God, and, in that same mysterious moment, find our true selves.

Diving from the high dive is as good an image of prayer as it is of service. Prayer and service are what faith does, and both take us more deeply into those places where God can be discovered. Not only is God found by looking inward but, taking our lead from the Gospel, we also believe that God is just as significantly at home in the materially poor and the poor in spirit.

There are those among us who are systemically held in poverty, subjected to injustice, and deprived of education and political clout. As individuals, communities, and churches we find ourselves frequently mixed up in the social sin of callously walking past their needs. This kind of sin demands as much repentance and firm purpose of amendment as does our personal sin. But prayer and reflection teach us over time how the personal and social dimensions of our lives overlap and finally become one in the life we share with the Lord.

Learning to dive off the high board, however, comes with its own dilemmas. We risk becoming indiscriminate in our diving, not making an informed decision about which board is best for us to dive from. And what pools should we dive into? Pools can be filled with different kinds of water: chlorinated, salt, fresh, cold, or warm. In which pool will God take us aside and teach us how to really swim and dive? That's our place of service, our place with the Lord in ministry.

Finding that right pool, even with God's help, can be as daunting as it is complicated and occasionally confusing. That's when discernment becomes indispensable. We know we're in the right pool only when we see where it takes us—toward or away from God. Luckily, holy men and women have found their way to God before us and stand ready to help. We, too, need the Mr. Pope of our souls to guide us.

Let me tell you about Sarah, a good friend, a discerning companion in spiritual growth, and somebody who often brings me to Jesus. This usually happens when she cuts my hair, something she's done for almost twenty years.

Some people consider a haircut a bother, but I look forward to it. Vanity undoubtedly figures in my anticipation. I like changing my appearance, and I'm always going from longer to shorter hair, from highlights to lowlights and back again. But seeing Sarah is the real reason I look forward to haircuts.

Her father, a retired preacher, still seems vocationally compelled to point out his daughter's erring ways. Her Bible college education was short-lived, her abrupt departure politely labeled a "deep-seated difference in theological perspective."

Haircuts give us time to catch up. Sarah is always reading, and Flannery O'Connor is one of her favorite writers. Actually, her salon could qualify as a setting for a Flannery O'Connor story. A statue of the Little Flower is in one corner and Our Lady of Fatima stands guard in the other while, next to the sink, Jesus points to his Sacred Heart. A gigantic black rosary is draped over the mirror, and her scissors are housed in a tabernacle she found in an antique store. She's not Catholic, but there's no hint of ridicule in any of her display of Catholic devotion, only curiosity laced with reverence.

I once showed up early for an appointment, so I leafed through the paper and read my horoscope to kill time. "Be sure and don't get stuck in rigidity, but flow if you want to be happy," it announced. I smirked, duly noting the warning.

Taking my horoscope to heart, I decided to make a frontal attack on rigidity. "Just buzz it all off," I said.

"OK, we'll start at a half-inch and work our way down," she said.

Both of us were experiencing big life changes. I had just lost a corporate job in career management, and helping others through change felt nobler, or at least easier, than going through it myself. I'd actually been in the job too long, but safety defended me against boredom, something we usually understand only in retrospect. I needed a change but, just like all of us, I resisted being changed.

"I'm not built for another corporate job," I said to Sarah, "but being on my own is no picnic either. I'm probably just scared to make a decision," I finally admitted, as hair disappeared. Then I asked how her son's surgery had gone.

"Not well," she admitted. "The steroids Max has been on ate away at his hip, and the replacement surgery was a bust. How many twenty-year-olds need hip replacements? It breaks my heart to watch him. He doesn't need this." I just nodded.

Max was diagnosed with leukemia about the same time Sarah's younger son started setting fires at school and went kicking and screaming into drug rehab. He's been through rehab a couple of times since then, but Sarah hopes this time he'll stay clean and sober. She's no stranger to heartache, but I've never seen her without hope or humor, and that's strengthened me over the years. She's been beaten up by hardship but never beaten down, backed into a corner, but never hopelessly boxed in by despair.

When my hair was close to stubble, Sarah said she had an idea for me. "OK; I'm all ears," I said. "Tell me."

"You know," she said, "I think God wants to take you on a field trip into life; you just need to get on the bus." Then she laughed a little and added, "But stop waiting for your mommy or daddy to sign the permission slip so you can go."

My horoscope seemed suddenly superficial, but Sarah's punch line had the intimate feel of God's ever-fresh advent of grace, a glimpse into how I needed to live more graciously, freely, and faithfully.

I like to tell people that Sarah is my real spiritual director. After all, with just one quick comment, she showed me how playing it safe, while certainly predictable and even cozy, might not be how God desperately wants to introduce me to ever-greater life. She was right: I needed to give myself permission to get on the bus, see things I'd only heard about before, and finally find a new place to live for a time. In the end, fearful safety and predictability turns out to be tedious and boring, just like the corporate job I was afraid to leave.

Take some time to remember and then write about at least three people in your life, who, like Sarah in mine, have led or even carried you kicking and screaming to Jesus. How did they teach you about God? Have you thanked them for their help? We ought to, because these folks are our heroes in faith, for whom we need to be ever grateful.

Walter L. Farrell, S.J., was a faithful companion of Jesus for all of his ninety-six years. I knew him for forty-five of those years, and his death hit me hard, in part for an embarrassing, selfish reason. He had been a part of my life for so long that I just assumed he'd always be there to set me straight when I veered off course. His advice was always wise enough to be simple, insightful, and deeply compassionate. He was a friend of God, and, as the homilist correctly said at his funeral, you couldn't be in Walt's presence without feeling honored.

Walt was living in Washington, DC, years ago, when I tumbled into a professional and personal black hole. Faced with decisions that would affect the rest of my life, I flew to Washington from Detroit to spend a couple hours with him. With the benefit of hindsight, I see clearly now that I really wanted him to tell me what to do. A quick fix was all I thought I wanted, but that's not what I got.

As I remember, I ranted and raved for at least an hour but, when I finally finished, Walt just paused, took a deep breath, and asked a simple question. "Have you ever had a room where no matter how many times you rearranged the furniture, nothing ever really seemed to fit?" I nodded, letting him know I had. "You can try to force it into the room or get new furniture," he went on, "but that might not take care of things either." Another pause, one more deep breath.

"Sometimes," he suggested, "the furniture isn't the problem. The real problem is the room. Redesign the room and maybe you'll have a fighting chance of things fitting." That was enough. I thanked him and flew back to Detroit.

For years I thought Walt had simply taught me an important lesson about perspective, but I finally understood that he really taught me about discernment.

Maybe you've moved from a large house into a condo. For some reason, most people who do so—my mother included—believe thirty years of accumulated furniture ought to fit perfectly into the new space. That's the having-my-cake-and-eating-it-too syndrome. It's only after we stumble over furniture one time too many that we give some away or sell it.

I don't know about you, but I've had plenty of practice doing the same thing in my spiritual life. Our culture and even our churches want us to believe that the acceptable resolution to problems is that everything finally works out in the end. That's why we love situation comedies: No matter how much trouble the characters get into, all the loose ends are tied up with a bow at the end. But we don't live in situation comedies, and occasionally the only resolution to difficulties is finally accepting the fact that things just aren't going to work out. We need a new room.

God offers us help sorting out the furniture, and, when necessary, helps us design and move into new rooms. Start to get serious about spiritual growth, and we're all soon confronted with accumulated habits, attitudes, behaviors, and points of view that clearly clash with the new room God is building for us. Sometimes we're so attached to them, thinking we'll certainly die without them, that we try to hold onto and grow in God's life at the same time—the having-my-cake-and-eating-it-too syndrome.

Sooner or later, however, our spiritual growth comes to a grinding halt. Getting stuck like that is a sure sign that not all our furniture is going to fit in the new interior space God is building for us to live in. Sell some of it, or just throw it out, but something has to give.

Just like the rich young man in the Gospel (Mark 10:17–31), Jesus looks at us with love, but we also occasionally walk away sad. "Anything but that," we plead. Cosmetic changes are easy, but what we need is a change of heart.

We've all faced difficult times when making changes was not enough: Our souls needed to live in a new space. It happened to me when I finally had to admit that my vocation was not being a Jesuit priest. You may have experienced the same thing when, no matter how much you hoped against hope, your marriage came to an end, or a job you thought you'd have for the rest of your life became no longer satisfying or rewarding.

These kinds of spiritual redesign projects are especially difficult because they don't come with detailed blueprints. That's when God and faith and personal integrity take on real flesh.

I've had two kinds of teachers in my life. Information dispensers make up the first group. Give me plenty of books and enough time, and I can do for myself what they purport to do for me. Their teaching is often deadening, rarely creative. But original insight is the business of the second kind, and that's something I can't do by myself. These teachers show us how to think and frame questions. This kind of teaching is infectious and empowering.

From what I've heard, Holy Cross Father John S. Dunne, long-time theology professor at the University of Notre Dame, belongs in the second group. Before computers took over course registration, students camped out all night to get a place in his classes. His teaching was consistently brilliant and highly intuitive, restless in its questioning, personally involving, even life changing. I regret he was never my teacher.

His books have the same feel. His trademark meandering way of poking at questions and dilemmas can be frustrating, but stick with it and you'll stumble onto insights that are so altogether jaw dropping in their genius that you'll have to put the book down to absorb the impact of what you've just read.

Long ago, in those primeval times before DVDs and podcasts, I listened to cassette recordings of retreat talks he gave to the Trappist monks of Gethsemani Abbey. At one point he chronicled how he drove from the Golden Gate Bridge to Notre Dame's fabled golden dome. Since I've also driven cross-country from San Francisco, I was familiar with the sights he described.

I also remember the seemingly endless ups and downs and twists and turns that are the agonizing fate of anybody who drives through the Rocky Mountains. But get out past Denver, Dunne comments, and everything changes. The topography abruptly turns flat, very flat, and the horizon appears to stretch on forever.

That's when, he casually mentioned, "All of a sudden, I knew I was looking at the rest of my life." Already in his late fifties, the sudden geographical monotony showed him that from then on, most of his personal and spiritual growth would happen below the surface, underground, out of sight.

Isn't the first half of our lives devoted to navigating legitimate external challenges: climbing the generative mountains of achievement in work, stability in relationships, and religious devotion? But the kids finally move out, the promotions stop coming, and somebody we trained becomes our boss. Try for a new job and we're judged to have too little energy, be too expensive, or too rigid — just too old. That's when we face a new question: Is there true life for us after success?

I have a friend, an accomplished sales executive in his late fifties, who's been unemployed for two years. When we last talked, he was running out of money fast and needed to hatch an alternate reemployment plan even faster. He'd had a couple interviews but received no job offers. Mixed with his panic, however, was the shadowy outline of new freedom, often the gift of shifting perspectives. Now he's looking for a job that supports his life rather than defines it.

Finding life below the surface is a challenge at every phase of life. Think of when the magic just seemed to disappear from a perfect marriage, or when our dream job turns out to be just another job. Think of how we struggle to keep praying when it no longer feels warm and comforting, or when our much-loved, long-anticipated first baby decides to cry all night, every night. Each of us has our own experience. Lurking just below the surface of all our experiences are opportunities for growth and grace when we give ourselves over to the miraculous drudgery that marks the humble service of love.

You and I live in between the challenges of crossing our personal Rockies and the apparently uneventful monotony of life east of Denver. Luckily, our God sticks with us in the heights and depths of life. After all, Jesus was resurrected after spending three days in the earth's embrace, and when we stay close to Jesus below ground—in the earth—impasse can give way to possibility, death to resurrection, drudgery to glory.

Although we're constantly called to live out the grace that bridges life above and below the surface, this call comes with a particularly acute poignancy as we age. That's when we're called to travel east with God, way out there, beyond Denver. We can't afford to forget that the new light of our daily resurrections also dawn out there. And in this case, that's when we can come to see that the light of all our dawns shines forth from our Eternal East.

I just got off the phone with my thirty-year old nephew, Brendan, who's sitting in the Cincinnati airport with a one-way ticket to Cairo, Egypt, in his pocket. He's had enough with the "arrogance of capitalism," as he describes it, and wants to feel the energy of a society rebuilding itself.

Two years ago, my twenty-something friend from Malaysia, Rooney, left home to live in Germany, without a job or much knowledge of the language. He was tired of trying to live as a young gay man in an Islamic country, always hiding, pretending, and fearing.

Both remind me of my parents when they were twenty-something and packed us all up in a dark brown DeSoto and moved from Philadelphia to rural Ohio. Once we arrived there, dad got busy building his medical practice, I started school as the only Irish kid in a sea of broad-faced, blond-haired kids with names like Scheckelhoff, Stechshulte, and Schmiedebusch, and mom cried hanging up laundry in the backyard, begging God for just five minutes at the corner of Fourth and Chestnut back in the City of Brotherly Love. I took the move in stride, but Mom and Dad always felt out of place in Ottawa, Ohio, the self-proclaimed Soybean Capital of the World.

I lived in a city for the first time when I started college in Detroit, and I was exposed to people of color there for the first time. Graduate school followed in New York, and people there scared me. They were direct and gruff, if not conceited, and I often felt like Jethro

Bodine staring at all the tall buildings in the big city. But I soon felt comfortable there, and, to my great surprise, did well in school and lived on the East Coast for many years.

Taking all these transitions to heart, I got a sense of what Jesus must have felt like when, as the Gospel says, he came out of Galilee. After an apprenticeship with John the Baptist and forty days wandering in the desert, he set his eyes on Jerusalem—his Cairo, Germany, and New York. All the while, his burning sense of mission was sustained and enlarged by a deepening sense of intimacy with his God, the sustaining presence he called "Abba."

Maybe "coming out" is a good image of our life with Christ. Not only did Jesus come out of Nazareth into a larger world, the people he touched came out of sickness and even death into startling new ways of being alive. When Jesus finally came out of the grave into a dazzling redefinition of life, all our transitions from narrowness to largeness and death to life finally find a story big enough to hold them all.

Some of our coming out stories involve moving from one place to another. But there are others that tell how we made it from isolation to community, and from selfishness to the paradoxical fullness of self-forgetting. Sometimes we get a fleeting moment of transfiguration, when we get a privileged peek at the glory hidden in it all. But most of the time grace happens and God smiles when we simply embrace our day-to-day lives over time, with all our grace-treated will.

From time to time I imagine my life with God is an unfinished novel called—you guessed it—My Coming Out Story. What if you took time to imagine the same thing? If you did, what would your novel be called? What would you call the chapters? How would you decide when one ended and another began? Who are the main characters? What's the theme of the story? How does it end? What does the person who writes the introduction say about you? But most important of all: What would you hope they could say about you?

I'm hoping Brendan will find the life he's looking for teaching English in Egypt, but I know Rooney is successfully carving out a life for himself in Wuppertal, Germany. And, all things considered, I'm doing OK in Minnesota.

Our family loved the old DeSoto that moved us from Philadelphia to Ohio, but we finally traded it in for a new Oldsmobile Holiday 88 Coupe. Trading in old places and worn-out parts of ourselves introduces us to the worlds of grace that just keep getting bigger and bigger.

I remember reading a story about an ancient Japanese samurai warrior that remains as emotionally alive for me today as when I first read it. The warrior saw his master killed in battle, and the samurai code of honor required the warrior to avenge his master's death and preserve his dignity by killing the killer.

Many years later, the warrior finally tracked down the killer. As he approached him, he drew his sword, prepared to carry out the fatal revenge that honor required. But before he could kill him, the man spit in the warrior's face. The warrior instantly put his sword back in its scabbard and bowed deeply to the killer before he calmly walked away.

You may be straining to understand the story, just as I did the first time I read it. The warrior, I've come to understand, was thrown into a rage when the killer spit on him, and if he had killed with all that anger running through his veins, he would have been acting from anger rather than honor. His motive was no longer pure, and he had to walk away.

The story might help us better understand the Christian notion of purity of heart, a way of living that has remained a staple in Christian spirituality from the Gospels to the sayings of the desert monastics, from St. Benedict in the sixth century to the philosopher Søren Kierkegaard in the nineteenth. Kierkegaard described purity of heart as willing one thing, and in that description we hear echoes of the

Gospel mandate to "strive first for the kingdom of God" (Matthew 6:33). Mixed motives have no place in the hearts of the followers of Jesus.

And then there's my heart, and maybe even yours. More often than I like to admit, my motivation to do or not do something is mixed at best, seldom as selfless and focused as the Gospel admonition. Luckily, it looks like we're not alone.

St. Paul wrestled with the same thing, admitting that, "I do not understand my own actions. For I do not do what I want, but I do the very thing I hate…. But in fact it is no longer I that do it, but sin that dwells within me…. For I do not do the good I want, but the evil I do not want is what I do" (Romans 7:15, 17, 19). Doesn't this strike a familiar chord? Don't we feel a deep kinship with Paul? But what do we make of that something "that dwells within" us?

St. Ignatius Loyola has good advice to offer us as we wrestle with this question. One of the objectives of the Spiritual Exercises is "Preparing and disposing the soul to ride itself of all inordinate attachments, and, after their removal, of seeking and finding the will of God."

As we struggle to understand what really motivates us—a critical first step in grace-filled discipleship decisions—we need to understand which of our attachments are ordered and lead toward God, and which are disordered and finally end up leading us away from God. It may help us to think of these as our healthy and our toxic relationships with things, attitudes, persons, and behaviors.

Take some time and try to remember a real experience in your life when you acted on pure, Gospel-based motivation, and another time when you either knew or came to understand that you were acting under the influence of an attachment based in pride and ego. Write about how each of these experiences felt, not only when you did them, but later, after they stood up to the test of time.

Once we understand what disordered attachments are and how they function, most of us can feel the difference. That's why it's important to build up muscle memory of both. Most people can feel the difference, and our muscle memory guides us in future decisions. While you are reflecting and writing, is there one disordered attachment that frequently seems to grab you and pull you down? Only when you're conscious of what it is and how it influences us do you stand a chance of growing in faith.

These unhealthy, addictive behaviors and perspectives are often so chronic, so deeply engrained that we can easily miss them. This is another reason the examen prayer is so important. The critical importance of reflecting on both the positives and negatives of our day bring our motivations into clearer focus.

Remember that reflection is not analysis. Analysis picks experience apart, but reflection allows us to get a sense of the whole before we get dive into the details. The examen is a prayer, and like all our prayer, we never do it alone—only with the Lord. Alone and without God's loving help, prayerful reflection on the state of our soul can quickly turn into lonely, savage self-analysis. But God always works to preserve our honor.

Despite all my references to Starbucks, I'm actually an equal-opportunity coffee drinker. During the warm weather I like to pray early in the morning on the patio at Caribou Coffee. The traffic and conversation around me become white noise, and, after I put my feet up, I can watch the sunrise. I like to pray for people as the sun rises, hoping God will keep them safe in the dazzling light of our daily resurrections. It's also a good time to close my eyes and feel the consolation of God's warming gaze — after all, *consolation* means being "in the sunlight."

I remember one day when clouds overtook the sun, and things quickly turned dark and cool. It happens all the time, but that morning it taught me how different kinds of darkness can affect us for good or ill.

As I mentioned in an earlier story, we can be tempted to think that desolation, depression, and the dark night are all the same. They're actually quite different, and anybody wanting to grow spiritually needs to be able to tell them apart. Each represents a different brand of darkness, and while desolation is a temptation and depression is an illness, the dark night is a grace and comes from God. Watching the sun and clouds on Caribou's patio that morning showed me the difference.

When the clouds covered the sun, my first reaction was, "I was enjoying the sun's warmth; I want it back, now." I had little patience being without sunlight, the literal meaning of *desolation*. I knew the sun would eventually be back, but I didn't want to wait: I wanted to feel warm again right then. When the sun finally escaped from behind the clouds, it was a new sun, not the one that initially disappeared behind the clouds. Now in a higher place in the sky, it radiated a different kind of warmth.

Aren't there times when God feels close, active, and comforting, and, then, all of a sudden, God seems to vanish, leaving us alone in the dark? That's usually when we're tempted to try to retrieve our consoling experience from the past, to resuscitate it. We want the God who used to be there, and we frantically try to recreate the past, rather than look for a God who always comes to us from the future, transforming our nostalgic desire into new light and life. Resurrection is never resuscitation.

Depression, on the other hand, is just darkness without any hope of light. It is never from God. It's like looking at clouds covering the sun with no memory that the sun was ever there and no hope that it will ever appear. It feels like life always has been dark and always will be; past and future collapse into a painful present without hope.

We can't pray chronic depression away; instead, we need to reach out for the help we need to get free of its ruthless grasp, always fighting to keep ourselves from collapsing into angry darkness. While desolation is a temptation, depression is an illness that needs to be treated. Although God is always with us, even in depression, we can't see that clearly until we slowly crawl out of it.

But we do find God in the dark night. It's neither temptation nor illness, but grace. It's like watching the sun get covered by clouds and knowing—almost instinctively—that we have to move forward, not backward. The person in the dark night knows that past conceptions of God, self, and the way things are supposed to be are all in the process of a rebirth that can seem dark yet always carries a hint of new life and grace with it. In the dark night, darkness doesn't tempt us like desolation or bring us down like depression. Instead, its darkness, unknowing, and confusion are pulling us forward into God's silent, ambiguous, yet always healing future.

Not everybody working to grow spiritually will experience depression or a dark night, but all of us without exception will experience the back and forth between consolation and desolation. As a result, we need to know what these experiences are like, what they mean, and especially how to get out of desolation. The "Rules for the Discernment of Spirits" at the end of the Spiritual Exercises of Ignatius Loyola offer time-tested, practical guidance about consolation and desolation.

If you aren't familiar with the Spiritual Exercises or the Rules for the Discernment of Spirits, have somebody who is knowledgeable about the Exercises explain them to you. There are also books available on the Rules for the Discernment of Spirits, as well as on the Spiritual Exercises, that offer insights into the process. After a clear explanation, you'll start to understand the dynamics Ignatius describes and be better equipped to use the guidelines he sets out for managing them.

After I've done this with people I talk with in spiritual direction, our conversations change dramatically. Abstractions fall away, and the focus turns to the interior movement in the soul that can move us toward or away from God's life.

To keep me on the straight and narrow, I have two personal holy days of obligation each year, the day after Christmas and the day after Easter. "Day after" liturgies are blessedly simple, hushed, without frills—right up my alley. Since there aren't a lot of people in church on either day, I can hide out in a quiet corner, perfectly content behind a pillar, out of sight.

I imagine the same kind of hushed, even reclusive feel to John's version of the resurrection story, with Mary Magdalene walking alone to the tomb in the kind of silence that only comes in the dark moments just before dawn (John 20:1–18). Once she gets there, however, her heart is broken for the second time. The stone that kept the body of Jesus safe in the tomb had been rolled away. Not only had Jesus been killed, now his body is missing, possibly stolen.

When she lets the other disciples in on the news, their boss, Peter, and the mystical disciple that Jesus loved race to the tomb. It's the mystic, it seems, that leads the Church, here in the person of Peter, to places of startling, mystifying life. After Peter gets his fill of the empty tomb, the men hightail it back to the Upper Room to hide. Only Mary stays by the tomb, alone and weeping.

Mary weeps without hope faced with the death of Jesus and now his body's disappearance. She wants the body back and, until then, her grief remains inconclusive and desolate.

You and I know Mary's pain. Although missing bodies are seldom part of our daily routine, we have suffered desolate times when what usually consoles and comforts us seems to vanish, and we're left alone with raw grief tinged with anger, and an anxious desire to get back what until recently offered strength, sustained our faith, anchored our hope. God seems gone too, and we have no clue where God's been hidden.

Think about how the work we loved for so long suddenly turns sour, or the child we want to protect stumbles or even falls. Remember how prayer can suddenly, without warning, lose its allure, and all we do is watch the clock and think to ourselves: This agony has to be over soon.

When consolations vanish and desolation becomes our home, we can be tempted to react just like Mary, looking to the past for a solution, frantically trying to revive the feelings that once kept us safe and sure. Her abrupt conversation with the man she takes to be the gardener says it all: Don't tell me to stop crying; just tell me where you've put the body of Jesus so I can get it back.

Despite it all, she simply waits near the tomb, alone with her grief until the supposed gardener speaks her name. That's when she recognizes him as Jesus, coming to her from God's promised future with a pledge of inconceivable life, startling hope. That's also what we're called to do: spend enough time with our grief until we're pulled into that hushed split second when dawn finally appears with an assurance of a new way of being alive with our name on it.

Mary's experience in the garden near the tomb gives substance to desolation and consolation. If we keep our eyes fixed on her experience there, we stand a chance of catching a glimmer of what these words really embody.

Imagine for a second that Mary's transformation from desolation to consolation, grief to hope, and death to life doesn't happen quite so instantaneously. What if her tomb time turns out to be a metaphor for all the time it sometimes takes us—weeks, months, even years—to hear our name called so we can finally find our way out of the tomb's darkness and into the tentative dawn of true light—resurrection?

As Christians, we're called to do our "tomb time," like Mary, until our desolate sadness is not just taken away, but transformed and resurrected into the life of God. Our only hope is to wait patiently yet actively for Jesus to call our name and invite us into God's glorious future. When it's our turn, we also have to stand close to the tomb that turns out be our source of eternal life.

I love vampire movies. Even though I know they're packed with sexual and other assorted psychic overtones—maybe that's why I like them—I can't get enough of them. From the more traditional take-no-prisoners bloodsuckers of the past, to the hipper, softer types that populate contemporary blockbuster tales like the *Twilight* movies, I'll watch almost any vampire film, anywhere, anytime.

Just in case you're not up on the latest about vampires, here's a quick summary. Vampires are undead creatures who have sold their souls for a restless immortality that forces them to live in darkness and feed on the blood of others. They suck life out of their victims, and, in the process, turn them into vampires too.

Although they cower at the sight of crucifixes, and sizzle when holy water hits them, a wooden stake driven through their cold hearts is the only way to destroy them. That's when they're finally exposed to the light and their faces glow with the peace and serenity that evaded them for so long. They find their peace in being turned back into ordinary, mortal humans, free to die a natural death and finally rest in peace.

Vampires have certainly bitten me, and I'll bet they've also bitten you. Start working on spiritual growth, and they'll eventually reveal themselves lurking in the dark corners of our hearts. It's up to us to finally free them from their undead status, and allow them to turn back into mortal, fallible human beings. That's when we'll be freed from their grasp and able to live under our own power—finally.

Take some time to identify and then write about the vampires in your life. In other words, who are the people, or events, or mind-sets —from the past or the present—that still exert morbid, belittling, and smothering authority in your life without your permission? To whom or what have you granted immortal status?

Take it from me, these ghosts are always at work in us, often unconsciously, checkmating us at every turn, constantly dictating how we think about ourselves, undermining our own personal power, and keeping us from entering into the freedom that is the Spirit's gift to God's people.

Let me give you an example. There are people in my life in whose presence I involuntarily revert to scared-kid status, with precious little independence and even less confidence. I'll always be grateful for the ways I learned to be alive from my parents but, like many of us, I've spent a good deal of adult time working to unlearn the stuff I learned from them that still tries to dictate who I am and what I can do.

I recently attended a friend's funeral and found myself around people I hadn't seen in years. Within seconds we were relating to each other the way we did back then, and I could feel the old rivalries and insecurities rise to the surface once again. I had to keep myself from automatically giving away personal power to them.

Sometimes we give the Church too much authority, and we have to consciously reclaim our personal authority to make decisions of consequence for ourselves. Allowing people, institutions, and points of view to influence us is one thing, but giving them power to dominate us is quite another thing.

When we sacrifice our freedom and personal power in relationships like these, we find ourselves too often on the side of childish deference rather than adult decision making, control rather than loving influence, and incapacitating fear rather than the freedom given to God's friends. How can we escape reckless domination by institutions, points of view, and people determined to make us mere extensions of themselves? Only in the wood of the cross passing through our hearts. That's when we find freedom and our vampires find peace.

Our hearts find peace in the wounded heart of Christ. Against the background of the death and resurrection of Jesus we can confidently hand over our hearts without fear of seduction and abuse. It's only at the foot of the cross that we can see others for who they have always been: fragile, imperfect, and altogether mortal bearers of the kind of life we can only call eternal.

After the cross does its work, we can finally stand shoulder to shoulder with all the people in our lives who look forward to the true immortality of resurrection. I sometimes wonder about how deeply sad my parents and others would be if they ever knew the kind of power I once handed over to them. In the end, all any of us can hope for is to find the kind of real life and freedom that is our gift only in the humble wood of Christ's cross.

I like to pray early in the morning (some call it the middle of the night), sitting in the big, overstuffed brown leather chair in my living room. When I sit there, I feel as though I'm being held in strong, sheltering arms, the way I hope to feel when I pray.

From this chair I look directly into my office. My desk is cluttered with piles of half-finished work that like to give me the evil eye when I'm praying in the other room, and a nagging compulsion to get busy and be productive comes over me when I catch a glimpse of all that work screaming for attention. My place of activity threatens battle with my place of prayer.

But all that stuff looks tamer, less judgmental, even less demanding when seen in silence. That's also when I feel best equipped to respond to it all calmly and freely, rather than reacting in spiteful panic, out of psychological breath.

Seeing things in silence is a good image of the examen prayer. Sit in silence long enough, open to God's own holy silence, and we start to see what things look like through God's eyes. When we see things this way, some things are clear occasions of grace, but others will inevitably move us away from grace, sometimes at full speed, other times with a slower, more calculating, even more insidious pace. But we also see things in silence that we're not sure whether they come from God or from ego. That's when things can get dicey, and the examen prayer becomes a must.

Give God a split second to open our eyes and help us see clearly, and we get a running start on all that "not sure" stuff. Then we stand a chance of seeing what stuff belongs to God and what might lead us down the all too familiar path of pride and compulsion.

It takes a long time, doesn't it, to silence our fear of silence? When we finally figure out that we won't die if we fail to fill up all our silent space with kinetic thoughts or compulsive activity, God can help us see silence as a permanent, welcoming part of all experience, maybe even a divine silence that is the grace-soaked background of all God's creation, including ourselves. Prayer opens us up to God's life stirring in the silence that envelops us and holds us close. Fail to embrace it, and we run away from God—and self.

Here's a suggestion for how you might occasionally pray the examen. Once you've found your place in God's holy silence, make a list of the top three things that are screaming loudest for your attention. Then ask God's help in listening for those quieter voices in you, the ones that risk getting drowned out by the others.

Look at everything in the freedom of God's silence. Wait until all the interior screaming and yelling dies down; which voices then speak to you with the calmer authority of God's voice? What might God be asking you to notice, learn from, act on? What might we see that is familiar or a surprise? Remember that God's voice calls but never compels. The examen prayer doesn't have to be all work, either. Give God time to love you and for you to love God back.

On the way back to prayer one morning, after refilling my coffee cup, for some reason I stopped in my office, sat in my desk chair, and looked back at the leather chair in the other room. A different perspective, I thought, perhaps even a different focus for examen prayer. What does the place of prayer look like from the place activity? Even more important, how do they form and inform each other? What does the tension between contemplation and action look like, and how is it resolved?

I doubt that tension is ever fully resolved, but we find peace and our life in God's spirit in learning to live in the ambiguous space between the two, content to be pulled in one direction and then the other. Learning to balance the two can become our grace.

Have you ever watched a tightrope walker use a balancing pole? Balance, it turns out, is always dynamic, and the pole enables the tightrope walker to counterbalance a pull in the opposite direction. Isn't this what happens when we pray?

Whether I'm looking at work in silence or looking back into silence from work, God helps me slowly learn how to see from both perspectives—both chairs—at the same time. Silence and activity complement and complete each other, and finding the balance between the two is God's precious gift.

How Happy Can God Be?

"No, not a chance. I don't think he could be." That's the answer I received without asking from the clerk who sold me the book *Is God Happy?* by the late Polish philosopher Leszek Kołakowski. "God can't be happy when he looks down on what man does. That's $31.20 on your Visa." I picked up the book, took back my card, and told her I'd let her know what this guy thinks.

The clerk's comment and Kołakowski's question got me thinking. Luckily there was a Starbucks in the bookstore, so I popped in and read part of my new book as I sipped iced tea. By the time I had something to report, the clerk was gone for the day.

Kołakowski's image of God—similar to images of God we've explored together in this book—is of no abstract being, no eternally unchangeable, uncaused cause somewhere out there building divine sandcastles in a philosopher's sandbox. Instead, God has become incarnate and shares our life. But the God we see in Jesus endured the brutal assault of pain, hate, and death we all share. How could God be happy after all that?

And how can we be happy? After all, we share a common humanity with Jesus, filled with pain and the ultimate prospect of death. Is happiness simply a welcome pause in our pain? Is it what David Foster Wallace called one of our favorite "technologies of escape"?

We live, however, in hard-won faith, hope, and love that knows suffering and death, but refuses to be defined by darkness or destruction. Resurrection is no escape from death. Instead, our faith assures us and our experience teaches us that death is finally and forever transformed in the life we share with God in Jesus, and in the courageous power of the Holy Spirit.

Once again we run into the experience of spiritual binocularity, an important metaphor of this book. Don't death and resurrection come to us as one inseparable experience of transformation in God's life? Don't we live perpetually suspended between our wounds that are never fully healed and an offer of grace that is never fully lived, certainly never exhausted? After all, there's more to God than the humanity of Jesus, and there's more to our lives than only suffering and death. We live in the glory of this hope. That's what I hope we've been able to explore together in *Startled by God*.

The really significant stuff—God, love, forgiveness, joy, friendship, thanksgiving—are always invisible and visible at the same time. The give and take between what's seen and unseen is what makes our relationships with God and others so compelling, even startling.